WHAT HAS
ULTIMATE RELEVANCE ?

In Plain Language

BY
MARK C. PLAIN

PLAIN PHILOSOPHY CENTER, PUBLISHER
RICHMOND, BRITISH COLUMBIA
CANADA

WHAT HAS ULTIMATE RELEVANCE?
Copyright © 2006 by Mark C. Plain.

Artwork, Page 19: courtesy of NASA Ames Research Center, California

Library and Archives Canada Cataloguing in Publication

Plain, Mark C.
    What has ultimate relevance? : in plain language / by Mark C. Plain.

Includes index.
ISBN 0-9739488-0-9

1. Relevance (Philosophy). 2. Relevance logic. I. Title.

B105.R3P53 2006   160   C2006-900040-9

CONTENTS

QUESTIONS & ANSWERS CONTENTS

**This book is dedicated to
all the Angelical at Heart.**

Introduction

"Truth above all, even when it upsets or overwhelms us"
Henri Frederic Amiel

W hat is the purpose of life? Why are we here? Is all that has been seen, all that can exist? These grand questions have been with us from time and memorial. They are considered by many astute people to be our deepest philosophical conundrums, because the answers can only be found at the top-most and bottom-most scales of the Universe.

Consequently, those who seek for the solutions must be willing to struggle through a long cerebral journey of shifting premises, alluring mirages of subjectivity and quantum leaps.

To avoid tripping over themselves or wandering in circles, they must habitually re-assess the nature and limitations of their wisdom. As a result, traveling on the high road of objectivity is not easy. I know, because as a philosopher, I've chosen to undertake this expedition.

Currently, I'm happy to report that I have discovered a open area of very sobering *greener grass,* which I now feel compelled to share with others.

My Journey

My journey began years ago with an innate desire to learn the full complement of options that life has to offer me. (Not only the conventional assortment, but also all the hidden opportunities that one might dare to dream about.) To secure this full list, I realized early on that I first had to determine what was possible and not merely plausible, even if that meant starting from scratch.

My first strategic plan was to initiate a scientific undertaking to acquire immortality, hence, particles physics became my first love. However, after years of analytical investigation,

I got bogged down by many, widely-held scientific premises, which on closer inspection, turned out to be dubious—at best.

Soon afterwards, I had a classic "near-death experience," which caused me (for the first time in my life) to doubt my atheism. I found myself quietly drifting into the Philosophy of Science and Christianity and No! this discipline is not an oxymoron.

After many years of inquiry and philosophical contemplation into this new field, I began to recognize a very rich and exquisite tapestry of trans-woven concepts and ideas. I also found many fascinating connections, which challenged my preconceived notions and expanded my imagination about the unknown. I thought, what better way to itemize my new discoveries, then through answering the question, *What has Ultimate Relevance?*

You see, the criticism I hear most often about philosophy is that,

> "It's simply not relevant in today's world. Socrates, Plato, Aristotle and many other philosophers were very intelligent thinkers—but only for their time. They were not privy to our modern-day knowledge cache and therefore their ideas have only minor practical significance." (It's rather like saying, "the first computer operating system was essential, but now it is basically obsolete.")

To some extent, I would agree with this critique; however, philosophy is not shackled or indentured by it's past devotees, i.e., we shouldn't throw the baby out with the bath water. Also, consider this very practical line of reasoning.

Ask anyone if they would like to have their ideas widely published for free. Most people would be delighted with the proposal. However, if you insist that it's an *"all or nothing deal,"* namely, they must submit all their notes, including everything from high school and college—you will get a very different reaction. They will request permission to perform a *serious* editing job on their old writings, before they can feel fully comfortable in releasing them. This is because they no longer support many of their old ideas for reasons of irrationality, incohesiveness, political incorrectness, and above all, naiveté (lack of objectivity). In some cases, they would feel embarrassed to associate their name with such an ill-digested book. This is an unfortunate "consequence" and sign of intellectual maturity.

I don't believe that this generation would be unique throughout history in wanting to make this type of editing request. If we could somehow, bring back Aristotle today and query him on his views on "crystal spheres in the heavens," I have little doubt that he would disavow them, or want to revise them faster than anyone can say, "cosmological constant."

Everyone routinely updates various ideas that they have previously acquired. So, why should anyone from the 4th century BCE be any different? Why should we assume by default, that Aristotle would change nothing, simply because he's yet to make the request? Who should have the burden of proof, given the fact that there is no evidence, either way?

Modern-day common sense might suggest that every idea should be forced to *sink or swim* based on its own merits and not given a free pass due to it's pop-origins. Maybe then we can begin to herd the *sacred cows* of the past and adopt a more skeptical perspective on the nature of reality. This has always been my approach.

As you may have noticed, my writing style is somewhat condensed. I like to get to the heart of the matter quickly and concisely. Fortunately, this approach has not hindered me from briefly covering all the main junction points of my philosophical journey. I hope you enjoy the ride.

To play it safe, I will begin with a blank slate. I know this may sound fairly laborious, but sometimes our preconceived notions can get in our way, i.e., false premises can be very problematic.

CHAPTER 1

Premise

"It's not the things we don't know that get us into trouble; it's the things we do know that ain't so."
Will Rogers

All our current knowledge is founded on specific premises, which are in turn based on even deeper primary premises. This raises the obvious question (and good starting point)—does the Universe have an objective, irreducible, irrevocable fundamental premise, and if so, what is it?

Well, let's start with the most basic entity in the Universe, which is empty space. What is the smallest or fundamental volume of empty space? This is not a scientific question, but rather a philosophical one.

Empty space maybe infinitely divisible

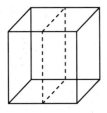

Figure A

Picture a volume of empty space— any size. **(Fig. A)** Cut it in half. Take one of the two remaining sections and cut it in half again. If you continue this series of dissections, the volume of the remaining space will get smaller and smaller. Ask yourself; is it possible to continue these divisions indefinitely? What evidence is there to rule out this possibility? Answer: There is no conclusive evidence. Half of any volume greater than zero maybe yet, another volume greater than zero. Accordingly, *there maybe no such thing as the smallest volume of empty space.* I.e., we maybe living in a "bottomless" Universe in all directions, with little infinitesimals everywhere we look. (This is my fundamental premise.)

Now consider the other side of the cosmic scale. Is there a "top" to the Universe, such as a barrier or wall at the outer limits of outer space?

Pragmatically speaking, for the past 400 years every time astronomers and engineers have built larger telescopes, they have found a larger cosmos and who is to say that this trend can't continue—*indefinitely*. There is no evidence that rules out this possibility either. Our Universe maybe "topless," i.e., infinite in all outwardly directions. It maybe possible to get into a rocket ship and travel in any collinear direction forever and ever.

Another important premise is that, ***there maybe no such thing as the smallest or fundamental particle of matter.*** Matter itself maybe infinitely divisible, i.e., every particle in the Universe maybe comprised of an infinite number of subparticles. Even if we can't see every one of these possible subparticles today, that doesn't prove that they can't exist. It may only prove that we haven't developed the perfect particle detector yet. Therefore, "absolute nothingness" is a purely abstract construct. To prove its existence empirically, one must first presuppose a bottom to space; however the veracity of this premise is exactly what is at issue here.

Another important premise is that, ***there maybe no such thing as the smallest or fundamental particle of life.*** No one can deny that we are made of hydrogen, oxygen, nitrogen, carbon, sulfur, phosphorous and some trace elements. But, how does one prove that we are *exclusively made* of these particle types? That, that's all there is to life? We really don't know enough about our entire subatomic spectrum to rule out any other significant mechanisms or subparticles. Life may have an infinite ingression of "living" substructures. Therefore, *there maybe no such thing as the smallest possible life form.*

Lastly, ***there maybe no such thing as the fundamental premise of knowledge.*** If the Universe is truly infinite (topless and/or bottomless) then all our collective human knowledge would be infinitesimal, relative to any infinite Universe. This will remain true no matter how much knowledge we amass, because discovered facts have a finite count. Therefore, we *might* be drowning in uncertainties right now and forever more. As long as we *might* be drowning in uncertainties, we will remain unable to determine the overall probability of this state, because there maybe a vast amount of data out there that we're simply not privy to. **Uncertainty always hides its magnitude.** For some, this is a very big piece of humble pie to swallow, but the Universe doesn't owe us anything. It doesn't owe us finitude. It doesn't owe us any answers—let alone certitude.

Hence, the acquisition of certitude and/or omniscience maybe unattainable. Our species may forever wander in the wilderness of the practical realm; never being able to define anything in true *absolute terms.* For example, some say that the sky is blue; that, that's an absolute, objective truth. However, the specific electro-magnetic frequency of sky blue, might have no last decimal place, so it is definable only in practical terms by rounding off to the nearest decimal place. **Nothing real in the Universe may have a last decimal place.** The very concept of finitude maybe nothing more than a human invention for reasons of practicality and commerce.

Without an objective, fundamental premise to knowledge, all our current "facts" maybe sitting on shifting sand. Everything we "know" about the Universe, maybe "yet to be revealed" superstitious nonsense. This human condition maybe unavoidable. Every generation maybe destined to stand on the shoulders of their forefather's knowledge, after which time, they are *filed away*—regardless of how deep their ideas were. Its like **everyone lives and dies encased in "amber," "trapped in time," like a prehistoric insect,** i.e., there is only a finite amount of accessible knowledge that anyone can possibly accumulate over their lifetime, regardless of which century they happen to be born into. And no amount of supportive evidence can preclude the future discovery of contrary evidence. Therefore, everything we know is at risk of becoming obsolete one day and that's just the way it is. We are either currently standing on the unshakeable bedrock of true wisdom, or merely riding another emaciated sacred cow through the quick sand of our own self-induced myopia. Relative to the absolute realm, there is no in-between state.

New Path

As such, as one pursues the answer to the question of *What has Ultimate Relevance*, they must first definitively determine whether or not, certitude is attainable. This new quest has become a necessary prerequisite. However, it also has its own prerequisite; namely, the survival of our species. This new "side detour" has objectively assumed *Ultimate Relevance* (provisionally speaking).

Many people feel that our species continuance is a given—a cakewalk, as we move forward. Unfortunately, nothing could be further from the truth. Terrorism and worse, Megalomania, will become exponentially more unmanageable in the future. The good news is that there is a solution to these serious threats, *albeit an unconventional one.* Once we get past this detour, we can resume with our main quest.

CHAPTER 2

Terrorism and Megalomania

"Technological progress is like an axe in the hands of a pathological criminal."
Albert Einstein

What is the solution to the problem of Terrorism and Megalomania? I will refrain from the usual buzz slogans like "re-doubling our efforts" or "having a heightened state of vigilance." These maybe helpful in the short term, but the long-term solution requires much more philosophical ingenuity.

Before I begin, I feel it is very important to clarify the full scope of this problem, because it is much more difficult to solve then it first appears. (Fortunately, since my solution is the same for both, I will focus only on Terrorism—to help simplify things.)

To start with, ***three major obstacles*** must be overcome in order for us to achieve success.

The first hurdle is *Terrorist Anonymity.* Simply put, we don't know for sure who the Terrorists are among us. Worst-case scenario, they could be solitary and morbidly reclusive individuals with no paper trail or any other overt evidence by which we can distinguish them—before they commit their act. (A network of one, if you will.) We shouldn't assume that all future Terrorists will be sloppy or impulsive and make it easy for us to detect them. It would be helpful if there were a specific gene or other biological marker, that we could easily test everyone for; but to date, none has been found.

On a much deeper philosophical level, even if we could force everyone to live in glasshouses, we can't overtly force them to live with a glass mind, which is why **a Big Brother type solution will never work.** The main reason is that the human mind maybe infinitely divisible, just like empty space, therefore it maybe unreadable by any external device. The more interesting question is this: can we *covertly entice* everyone to live with a glass mind?

The second obstacle is *Terrorist Cognitive Capabilities.* Terrorists are only limited by their intelligence, imagination and creativity, which are hopelessly unpredictable. For that reason, it is relatively impossible for us to be completely prepared for where or how they will strike in the future.

To analogize the full scope of this unpredictability, consider the life cycle of a typical computer virus. **(Fig. B)**

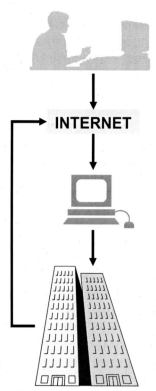

Cyber-Terrorists
coding a new virus called "Deep Creativity," to probe and circumvent their local installation of Anti-Virus Brand X, Y, Z, etc…

If successful, they may unleash their malicious code onto the Internet.

Unsuspecting Internet User
using Anti-Virus Brand X

First Viral Encounter = Victim

Brand X Anti-Virus Company
codes a new patch to detect and quarantine "Deep Creativity." It then auto-updates other Brand X clients, via the Internet, to help to ensure that there is **No Second Victim**

Figure B

Software viruses have been in general circulation now for many years—with no end in sight. Basically, the process starts when someone decides to write a virus. They install many of the latest and greatest anti-virus software packages onto their computer (on different partitions). They then begin writing their new virus code and test it against all these anti-virus packages, to see if it can be detected. If so, they will modify their code and through a series of trial and error processes, eventually render the anti-virus software ineffective. In most cases, this requires a lot of deep creativity—which is their main advantage over the static anti-virus packages. At that point, they can then upload the new virus to the Internet, where eventually someone will unsuspectingly download and execute it, claiming its first victim.

The most important fact that everyone needs to understand about anti-virus software is that, it will only protect your system from *"known"* viruses. This is a brand new virus; therefore, the first person to encounter it will invariably become a victim, regardless of which anti-virus package they have installed. Afterwards, this victim may decide to report the incident by sending a copy of their infected files to an anti-virus emergency center. These files can then be scanned for the *"signature"* of this new virus and then that signature will be incorporated into the next anti-virus upgrade patch—to help to ensure that there is *no second victim.* Nevertheless, **there will always be a first victim.** This nascent security gap has always existed. I call it the *first encounter strike susceptibility* or FESS for short. The very best the anti-virus companies can do is to play "catch-up," which is to react only after a virus has been detected, usually the hard way, i.e., only after it has been triggered and done its damage.

So, if you visit your local computer store you won't find a software package called the *"Very, very last anti-virus upgrade,"* despite the fact that it would be a multi-billion dollar product. Software companies can't create it, because they can't predict every conceivable future virus, that any conceivable future programmer can create. They simply can't foresee everything. It's like a medical doctor trying to create a vaccine to halt the spread of the next influenza outbreak, before anyone has become infected.

FESS maybe with us indefinitely and technically, it goes beyond just computer viruses. For example, in today's world it is possible to bring down a skyscraper with just a box cutter (as we discovered on 9/11/2001). ***Harmful creativity like all creativity is hopelessly unpredictable.***

The third major obstacle to eradicating Terrorism is the availability and capability of *Future Terrorist Tools*.

As technology relentlessly grows in scope and stature, our biological bodies remain the same size. Therefore, we are continually dwarfing relative to these newer technologies. Terrorists can exploit our escalating vulnerability by acquiring evermore-sophisticated tools, which can be used to unleash evermore-heinous deeds. As such, time is not on our side.

Today we have to be mindful of black-market uranium, nerve agents, designer pathogens, thermonuclear devices, prion agents, laser weaponry, radiological dirty bombs, RF armaments, missile technologies, chemical and biological weapons of mass destruction and I could go on and on.

It's only going to get exponentially worse in the future, especially after we develop and deploy gargantuan-sized space technology tools and equipment.

Space Colonization

If for no other reason than to avoid boredom, our creativity dependency will eventually force us to colonize outer space. **(Fig. C)** Our descendants will produce numerous space stations on the Moon, Mars and all the other planets in our Solar System. They will accomplish this by harnessing the massive quantity of interplanetary matter, which is basically free for the picking. They will expand their habitations in space, using countless other massive terraforming tools, such as lasers, masers, mass drivers and eventually self-replicating robots. (These are robot machines which can be placed on a variety of different soil types and transform it into perfect copies of itself.) If we assume a modest spawn rate of only one copy per month, per robot, **(Fig. D)** then the

Cutaway view - Toroidal Space Colony (see book cover)

Figure C

Time	Self-Replicating Robot Count
Start with	1
After 1 month	2
After 2 months	4
After 3 months	8
After 1 year	4,096
After 2 years	16,777,216
After 3 years	68,719,476,736
After 4 years	281,474,976,710,656

Figure D

production numbers become staggering i.e., there will be over 280 trillion robots after only 4 years. There is more than enough material in our Solar System to accomplish this—it is only a matter of time.

So, let us be very clear; **our descendants will be up to their necks in network linked, computer controlled, self-replicating robot machines.** Afterwards, these robots can be re-programmed to build trillions of other space tools. **Consequently, whoever controls these indifferent machines controls the Solar System and everything contained therein. In the hands of Terrorists, these indifferent machines can become virtual doomsday devices. In the hands of Megalomaniacs, they can create instant and endless dictatorships.**

In plain language, we are becoming increasingly more vulnerable to the potential created by our own advancing technologies and at some point a critical mass will be reached. I call it the **"Free Crown Point,"** (or FCP for short) because the first nation-state, or corporation, or individual to reach this stage, can Crown themselves as *"Ruler of the Solar System."* Everyone else will be so technologically marginalized by then, that they will be powerless to do anything about it.

Some people have speculated that there will be a *One World Government* installed before hand, which will ensure that it maintains absolute technological supremacy—at all costs. However, no government can know for sure, if it can implicitly trust every single one of its employees, not to steal their technology and instigate a *palace coup* with it. History has shown us repeatedly, that there is such a thing as a corrupt government official. Granted there have only been a modest number throughout recent history, but in the future, even one will become too many.

Rogue Egotist

Take a hypothetical case of an egotistical Megalomaniac who wants to be universally worshiped as a god by everyone—with or without their intellectual consent. He recognizes that he has full anonymity to patiently foment his ideas, inside his provisionally bottomless mind and look for creative opportunities to advance. He decides to work for this One World Government in the space colonies, because it offers him the best prospects. There is nothing to stop him from writing his own creative computer virus to infect a space based, computer controlled, laser installation. The FESS that all computers have, guarantees him at least *one clean shot* at it, i.e., if he can get his new virus into the laser's computer and get it to switch its *"allegiance"* to him; he can then use the laser as an offensive weapon to usurp supreme power over everyone else (and everyone knows it). This is the ultimate computer hack.

In future environments, everyone is only one computer virus away from attaining the Free Crown and there's no way to get rid of this susceptibility—no more than we can get rid of computer viruses or other forms of negative creativity.

In another plausible scenario, someone develops a brand new, superior *particle beam* technology in space. They decide not to tell—let alone sell it to anyone, because they ask themselves the basic question,

> "What could I possibly get in exchange for this technology that I can't already take by force—by using this technology? If I delay in exploiting this new advantage, then I run the risk of being bypassed by someone else's even better technology, tomorrow. Therefore, it is *use it or lose it time.*"

With new and improved inventions and technologies constantly emerging, at some point one of these inventors is going to say:

"Enough already, I'm tired of racing around like this. I want to use my currently superior technology to destroy everyone else's Research and Development departments. This way, I can ensure that my inventions remain number one, *indefinitely*—even if I have to impose draconian measures, e.g., global enslavement."

The dictum will be, ***"Whoever happens to have the biggest and best technology, can dictate all the rules."*** This includes everyone else's retaliatory capabilities—*if any.*

Overall Practicality

The overall practicality of this predicament is that, if we can't stop a first encounter strike, because of its inherent unpredictability and that single strike can wipe everyone out, via space lasers, self-replicating robots or other large tools on a whim; then why worry about any security measures in the space colonies. If we are involuntarily defenseless because of nature's limitations, then we might as well be defenseless. Why bother building the "Maginot line," if everyone knows that the "Ardennes Forest" security gap, is wide open to everyone—all the time. Therefore, **the Age of Space Colonization that is emerging will usher in the Age of Utter Defenselessness** (or AUD for short). It can be best exemplified by this statement, ***"a time where everyone will be at the mercy and pleasure of everyone else."***

So, to summarize; the three main obstacles to eradicating Terrorism are:

1. The innate privacy component from our provisionally bottomless mind. (They can easily hide their intent.)
2. The hopelessly unpredictable nature of negative creativity. (They can easily plan something new.)
3. The ghastly and unprecedented capabilities of ever-advancing technologies falling into the wrong hands. (They can succeed on their very first try.)

When we combine these three items, we end up with a *powder keg of instability*, which anyone can threaten to use on anyone else in the future. This means that there must be an unending promise by everyone, not to be harmful towards others. But, how do we verify such a promise—a priori? After all, the true Terrorists have a huge disincentive to be honest about this sort of thing (especially if they know that they can hide their true intentions.)

You see, the solution to the problem of Terrorism and Megalomania is much more difficult to solve then it first appears, because all our current provisional "solutions" expire at the Free Crown Point (FCP).

CHAPTER 3

The Solution to Terrorism

"Democracy is a terrible system of government,
except for all the rest"
Winston Churchill

A ll Terrorists and Megalomaniacs have only one universal flaw and that is; ***they happen to be stuck in the same boat with us.*** They have the same problem that we have. Just as we can't conventionally smoke all of them out because of nature's limitations, they can't smoke all of us out—*if we set it up properly.* I'm specifically referring to the creation and implementation of "Anonymity Biospheres" (or AB's for short). **(Fig. E)**

AB's are large terrestrial or space based habitats, each containing an isolated and self-determining community.

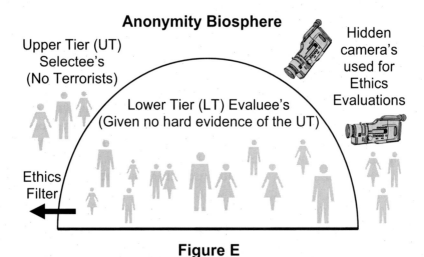

Figure E

Inside the AB's, everyone (from a young age) is raised in a very low-tech environment unaware of the hidden cameras all around them recording their every deed. **All future Terrorists and Megalomaniacs growing up in this type of environment will be unable to smoke out the fact that they are being videotaped and graded.** This is their *only common blind spot* and we have to *milk it* for all it's worth.

Some people feel that this type of solution is not practical or is too expensive or too time-consuming to implement. However, **no effort on our part maybe required.** This is because parenthetically, if we are going to build AB's on ourselves in the future—in order for us to survive ourselves—*then maybe we have already done it to ourselves!* Maybe this has already happened! There is evidence for this. **Yes, there is soft evidence of a highly advanced civilization of transcendent intelligences, using this planet as their AB.**

Before I explain this new soft evidence in detail, I want to point out that, if true, it changes our *landscape* significantly, in the following ways:

1. It validates the merits of the AB solution, vis-à-vis the problem of Terrorism and Megalomania, because if it is good enough for a more highly advanced society to utilize, then it should be good enough for us to utilize (should it become necessary).
2. If we are currently inside an AB, then there maybe no need for us to build our own future AB's, which will save us an enormous amount of effort, money and time.
3. We may not have to worry about the precariousness of the FCP anymore. However, it raises other questions, such as: how do *they* manage their society in the AUD? By what standards are we currently being evaluated? And how were these standards derived at—from purely pragmatic research?
4. They might teach us a lot about life, ourselves, the Universe and what has Ultimate Relevance.
5. (We might want to consider that only non-omniscient beings would use AB's.)

CHAPTER 4

The Soft Evidence

"What is now proved was once only imagined."
William Blake

I n order to make this soft evidence more philosophically obvious, it's best if we start off with an expanded imagination. After all, we are trying to understand the mind-set of a highly advanced culture.

We first need to comprehend their *motive* for deploying an AB, such as the Earth. This can easily be done, by us carefully extrapolating our future and then re-assessing our new standing from that heightened vantage point. This way our two civilizations will be on *common ground with common interests, motives and methodologies.*

To help to simplify this extrapolation, let us assume momentarily, that we are on our own in the Universe.

Fig. F is a projected timeline of future events.

As we move forward from the Terrorist events of 9/11/2001, ever-larger, indifferent technology tools will lead to further human marginalization and polarization between rich and poor. This will generate ever-greater fears and/or acts of evermore severe incidents of Terrorism and/or Megalomania.

Eventually the Free Crown Point (FCP) will be reached, causing wide spread anxieties and tensions. The *"Power Elites"* will be tripping over themselves to see whom among them, can don the Crown first and proclaim themselves as Ruler of the Solar System (Remember, it's *use it or lose it* time).

Extrapolation Timeline

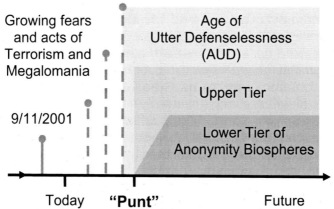

Figure F

During this time, the political establishment will become exhausted trying to manage this seemingly hopeless situation. Finally, after eliminating all conventional options, the politicians will decide to cut their losses, and *"Punt"*—for the good of the species. They will elect a commission of trusted, prominent moralists and charge them with the responsibility and oversight of AB construction and implementation. This commission will then begin the systematic introduction of young children and their support staff into the newly created AB's, for a future evaluation. *It would be child abuse, if they didn't do it.*

After some years, the commission will conduct their first and only batch selection of *evaluee's*. Their selection criteria will be based on very specific standards. Those evaluee's who are selected (*the selectee's*), will be brought out of the AB's into an *"Upper Tier,"* (or UT for short) and then given Supreme Power, including jurisdiction over all subsequent batch selections.

Those in the UT can then live out the rest of their years, free from the cameras and the fear of tyranny. Over time, I believe our civilization will migrate into this new two-tiered system.

Entrance Criteria into the Upper Tier (UT)

Continuing on with the extrapolation, how should we decide what the criteria should be for entrance into the UT? Filtering out the Terrorists and Megalomaniacs may provide the great impetus to initiate an AB/UT system, but should the "*Filter Threshold*," (or FT for short) be permanently placed there or should it be raised higher.

This question gets easier to answer when we consider the concept of adaptability. For example, if you climb to the peak of Mount Everest, you won't find a school of dolphins, because they are not well adapted to that specific environment. Likewise, the UT is also a unique setting, where all the selectee's must be innately predisposed to its new ethical and social surroundings—if they too are to survive—each other.

The major characteristics of the UT are:

1. *The Crown of the Solar System will be permanently and precariously within everyone's reach, free for the picking.* Therefore, any selectee with a scintilla of susceptibility to reach for the Free Crown creates an instant dictatorship.
2. There is **not a single security measure in place**, because there is no way to adequately predict all forms of negative creativity—so why bother. This is the AUD, where everyone will be at mercy and pleasure of everyone else's, governed by nothing more than their own conscience and common etiquette.

    Consequently, there will be no police, no courts, no jails, no passwords, no PIN numbers, no access codes, no keys, no locks, no anti-virus software and no laws, because *nothing is enforceable.* Everyone will have to trust everyone else with everything, indefinitely and unequivocally. Even as the population of the selectee's increase into the millions over time.

Think about it, most selectee's will be strangers to one another at first. ***How many strangers do you trust with just you PIN number***, let alone trust them with your life and freedom; let alone trust them with the Free Crown of the Solar System?

3. Our first UT will most likely be derived from our first truly permanent space colony, since Earth-based UT's are too susceptible to surgical air strikes and/or missile launches.

Given these three characteristics, the selectee's will have to be very unique individuals to survive each other. This is a very tall order. We need to ask ourselves a simple question, who can thrive in an environment with a permanent and precarious Free Crown? Lets be honest, it's the ultimate temptation. Who would be willing to give up the Crown? In exchange for what? Is there something else out there that's even more appealing? The answer is yes, there is—for some folks.

You see, the Crown symbolizes power and coercion because the only people who are susceptible to reaching for it, are those who are also willing to coerce others—or have a "will to power" over others. *The Crown is of no use otherwise.* Therefore, those individuals who are repulsed from the concept of coercion, will also be repulsed from the Crown and therefore can be trusted, "upstairs" in the UT. The ***opposite of coercion is Love,*** because it's our only attribute that can't be coerced *out of us.* It must be freely given by us.

To analogize this point, imagine that you come from a very close-knit family and you have all been invited to be the first inhabitants into a brand new UT.

In this situation, you wouldn't worry at all about the Free Crown, because you know that everyone upstairs will be a family member who loves you. (Some may find it easy to visualize this scenario.) So as long as there is a minimum common thread of mutual love running through everyone upstairs, the Crown becomes inconsequential. The fact that it's the AUD also becomes inconsequential. **Universal Love is the key to this whole thing.** Therefore, it has tentatively assumed Ultimate Relevance (provisionally speaking).

Safety Net

On a side note, it's possible to deploy a "safety net," to provide extra security. (**Fig. G**)

Chronologically speaking, we start off with our *"present world system"* and eventually build our first series of AB's—complete with evaluee's. Years later, we perform our first batch selection using a very stringent entrance criterion, which allows only *Quasi-Mother Teresa types* into our very first UT.

Afterwards they can be *"stepped up"* or educated in the use of contemporary technologies and philosophies. They alone can then build the first safety net. All they have to do is declare their UT, as a second level UT. All existing AB's become first level AB's, each with their own new isolated (low-tech) first level UT and unique entrance criteria (e.g. #1 and #2). This way if a first level entrance criteria turns out to be set too low and fails (e.g. #2), it won't affect the second level at all.

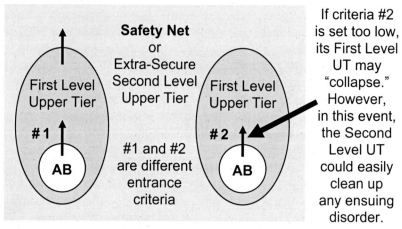

If criteria #2 is set too low, its First Level UT may "collapse." However, in this event, the Second Level UT could easily clean up any ensuing disorder.

Safety Net
or
Extra-Secure
Second Level
Upper Tier

First Level
Upper Tier

First Level
Upper Tier

#1

#2

AB

#1 and #2
are different
entrance
criteria

AB

Figure G

At the same time, the old *"present world system"* will:

1. Voluntarily isolate itself from all AB's and UT's.
2. Place itself under the jurisdiction of the newly chosen selectee's.
3. Allow its offspring to be transferred into the AB's for evaluation (under the supervision of the selectee's).
4. Eventually die out via attrition, leaving only a two-tier system of AB's and UT's, in its place.

Once a safety net is up and running, the selectee's can have a field day, playing around with all sorts of different entrance criteria, to see what pragmatically works and what doesn't work. Clearly, it will take longer to setup a safety net, but the benefits may make it worthwhile.

The Minimum Criteria

So, the minimum criteria will be set very high for our *first batch selection* into our first UT. This is because it is the *riskiest*—being a pre-safety net selection.

Accordingly, **we will select only those evaluee's who are completely enamored with the concept of Angelic Love towards all those who are like-minded—sight unseen.** Angelic Love includes righteousness (because nothing is enforceable upstairs), purity (to simplify matters) and also selflessness (a deep desire to support and grow the UT).

The fact that the selectee's might be strangers at first is irrelevant, because they all share the same love interest.

I recognize that Angelicalness is not everyone's *"cup of tea."* Lets be honest—it isn't. Figuratively speaking, some people like to eat broccoli and some people don't. Some people love to eat oysters and some people detest them. Some people want to live in a world where *Angelic Love is the preferred currency*, while others would prefer to wear the Free Crown. That's just the way it is and we just have to accept this fact. No one should feel compelled to provide excuses, because their decision is seemingly "irreducible," for all practical purposes.

I believe everyone's true values and desires are innate and can't be taught. *Only options can be taught.* Once a person **"finds themselves," i.e., who they really are and what they really want out of life**—they are set. This process can take decades to complete. I base this conclusion on personal experience and on the astonishingly high recidivism rates among many prison populations—despite all the education and counseling provided.

Generally speaking, we must respect everyone's autonomy (as far as they respect others autonomy). Even if that results in most people living their full lives inside the AB's and only a minority ever making it out into the UT, like Quasi-Mother Teresa types or those who think that Angelic Love is fun. These people really are out there and they are the best hope for our future. They may not be the most intelligent, or the most famous, or the best looking, or the most creative, or the most athletic, or the richest, but they have what it takes. They uniquely have no hard ceiling of mistrust and therefore can survive themselves effortlessly, in the utter fragility of the space colonies with a pervasive Free Crown.

We should be honest about this point, because the time will come when we will have to either ante up a better solution than the AB, recuse ourselves for the good of our species, or sign-up to become AB/UT facilitators. I see no fourth option on the horizon.

Anonymity Biosphere (AB) Filter Philosophy

Continuing on with the extrapolation, this is where my journey becomes a little "spooky."

You see, philosophically speaking, as we *"drill down"* into the inner workings of the AB, it becomes obvious that some type of filter will have to be circulated among the evaluee's.

This filter procedure is an essential tool to help the AB administrators (the selectee's upstairs) to better differentiate the evaluee's.

This AB Filter Philosophy must achieve (among other things) two main objectives:

1. It must instill a certain modicum of civility among the evaluee's or else anarchy will descend.
2. It must promote a culture of relative freedom, so everyone can freely choose from a wide selection of temptations. These temptations will act as virtual flypaper; helping the selectee's to determine the deepest desires of each evaluee.

Fascinatingly, when I began to write this overall AB Filter Philosophy, I quickly realized that it had already been written—immaculately. It's the Bible.

Aside from the question of whether or not God exists, it is clear that the Bible exists and this is part of the *soft evidence* that I was referring to earlier. However, for the sake of argument, let us continue to assume momentarily, that we are on our own in the Universe.

Let me give you a brief overview of how this AB Filter Philosophy might actually play out.

We build our first series of AB's, whether on the Earth or in space and populate them with a large number of children for the first evaluation. They are overseen by a support staff, sworn to secrecy. As the children grow-up, they are taught many things including language, reading, writing and the concept of the UT, *where all the Angelic adults eventually go.*

Once these children reach adolescence, many of the overseers will be secretively brought out of the AB's.

The next day we send in a hired stage actor to play the part of an Angelic messenger. (**Fig H.**) This is a person we dress-up in an angel-suit and lower him from the "ceiling" on these transparent strings.

When the evaluee's see this messenger descending they will

Figure H

be completely amazed. Remember, they have all grown up knowing only primitive technologies. We have deliberately set it up that way because we don't want them to know about our secret video cameras or hidden microphones. ***This is the ultimate reality show.*** Not only will all this equipment be out of their sight, more importantly, it will be out of their very imaginations (a truly covert type system).

When the messenger actor finally lands on the surface, he will proclaim to all the people saying, "I'm a messenger from the Captain of the UT. Let me prove it to you." He then whips out a small laser and proceeds to put on a laser light show. *"Ooh,"* the crowd will murmur. For his second proof, he pulls out a beaker of liquid nitrogen and dips a freshly picked flower into it. He then shatters the frozen flower over his knee to everyone's utter amazement. *"Whoa!"* the people will gasp. He then begins to read the Filter message:

> "Thus says the Captain of the UT; today I'm setting before you these commandments: Don't Murder, Don't Steal, Don't Lie, Don't be greedy, Spurn evil, Spurn any other messengers, etc. If you don't keep these commandments, you will receive individual curses. Conversely, if you do keep them you will receive individual blessings. If you keep all of them, *plus the optional bonus commandment*, you will be rewarded with the opportunity to move upstairs into the Captain's Mansion. The bonus commandment is to ***love your neighbor as yourself,*** not for who they are necessarily, but for what they might become (more selectee's). Give everyone some benefit of the doubt and believe the message I'm giving to you today—by faith, because I'm leaving. Good Bye."

Obviously, the messenger actor is not going to hang around for a lot of Q and A, because he can't inform the evaluee's why they are growing up inside an AB or why the Captain likes to play "hide and seek." That would defeat the whole purpose of the AB and the Filter message.

The messenger actor is then retracted back out of the AB and the evaluee's are left to ponder among themselves. They will whisper to one another,

> "What does this encounter actually mean? Who was that strange person—a wizard—an enchanter—or was he who he claimed to be, an Angelic messenger. Do I want to keep these commandments or not? What's in it for me? What are my feelings and values saying about all of this?

Each evaluee will have to grapple with all these questions (as well as others) and individually determine how they want to interpret the visitation. They will do so, based ultimately on their own innate desires, which is exactly why it was set up this way in the first place.

If an evaluee desperately wants to live in an Angelic environment, he or she will be prepared to exercise faith and believe the Filter message as-is—and act accordingly. After all, that maybe their only shot at true happiness. It would be too pessimistic for them not to believe the message. On the other hand, to those who have no interest in Angelicalness, they won't be inclined to believe the message and act accordingly.

Therefore, what we end up with is a lot of heavy moral grappling and a large granulated differentiation, based on each inhabitants true desires. Everyone above the Filter Threshold (FT) **(Fig. I)** is a true blue, selectee, destined for the UT.

These types of messenger visitations will go on periodically through out all subsequent generations, until the AB "bursts at the seams." This is when the evaluee's become too technologically advanced to be easily self-contained anymore. At that point, we must initiate a "second coming" event and start-up a brand new AB cycle, back at a technologically primitive state which can be easily controlled. These looping AB cycles can continue indefinitely across many AB structures—producing literally millions of selectee's. Bottom line, AB's are the best (if not the only) solution to eradicate the fear and acts of Terrorism and Megalomania.

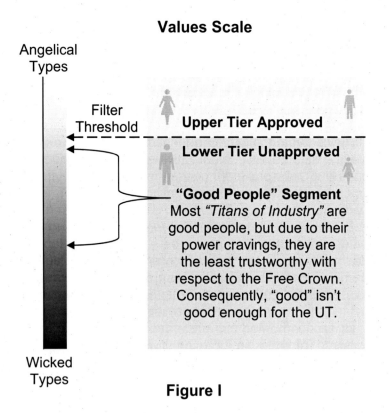

Values Scale

Angelical Types

Filter Threshold

Upper Tier Approved

Lower Tier Unapproved

"Good People" Segment
Most *"Titans of Industry"* are good people, but due to their power cravings, they are the least trustworthy with respect to the Free Crown. Consequently, "good" isn't good enough for the UT.

Wicked Types

Figure I

CHAPTER 6

GOD

*"God is love, and he who abides in love
abides in love, and God in him."*
John the Elder

After factoring in all the previous extrapolations, an obvious thought arises; **maybe God is one of us—** a transcendent intelligence who just happened to be among the first generation to run into the Free Crown problem years ago and ever since then we have been living inside God's AB, i.e., the Earth.

If it is true, then it maybe *the only game in town—* downstairs. Everything about us; everything we say and do maybe recorded and graded. This planet maybe nothing more than one of God's *nurseries,* specifically designed to find the Angelical (through incarnation). God may have no use for anyone else, since he can't ultimately trust them upstairs. Nor would he have any use for our primordial technologies and other shabby materialisms.

Metaphorically speaking, God maybe a kind of *"diamond" enthusiast,* who see's the Earth as a large automated mining facility. (Possibly one of many in his domain.) Like any good miner, God is willing to filter out *mountains of "dirt"* to acquire the true "gems," worthy of his bosom. Given his possible accessibility to trillions of self-replicating robots, much of his sifting operations can be pre-programmed and automated, so there is little reason not to set it up.

We are not going to find any hard proof of this scenario because if we ever did, it would defeat God's whole purpose for setting it up this way in the first place.

AB's must be covert to their evaluee's in order to yield fruit, i.e., successful bait cars, successfully hide their secrets.

The strongest piece of soft evidence available to us, are the parallels between the AB Filter Philosophy and the Bible.

The Parallels

If needs be, how many Biblical doctrines and teachings are we going to end up borrowing for our own future AB script? Well, I read from the book of Genesis to the book of Revelations and I can up with 20, covering virtually every major Christian tenet. Now I know what you are thinking—*time-out!*—that's just far too many coincidences—or is it? Judge for yourself; here are the 20 parallels:

1. The admonition to the evaluee's to be Angelic people. Love and Righteousness are crucial to the success of the UT and mandatory for God's salvation into his UT, namely Heaven. (John 13:35; "By this all men will know that you are my disciples, if you have love for one another." Also Rev. 3:15-22)

2. The use of brief Messenger visitations, to perform "miracles" to convey their authority and then to deliver announcements to the evaluee's such as moral commandments and other important instructions. (Exodus 24:12; Now the LORD said to Moses, "Come up to me on the mountain and remain there, and I will give you the stone tablets with the law and the commandment which I have written for their instruction.")

3. The use of rewards and punishments to those who choose to obey or disobey the commandments. The promises of "blessings and curses," a "Heaven" and a "Hell" to widening the evaluee's spectrum of temptations. (Deuteronomy 30:19; "I call heaven and earth to witness against you today, that I have set before you life and death, the blessing and the curse. So choose life in order that you may live, you and your descendants")

4. *The use of fulfilled prophesies.* After numerous AB cycles we will be able to easily anticipate and predict future events in subsequent AB cycles; similar to forecasting the life cycle of a commercial chicken. This technique helps to enhance moral grappling among the evaluee's. (Matthew 26:54; Jesus said, "How then will the Scriptures be fulfilled, which say that it must happen this way?")

5. The use of an Old and New Testament or multiple covenants. This is required to help micro-manage the ever-increasing sophistication of the evaluee's, from generation to generation. (Galatians 3:17; What I am saying is this: the Law, which came four hundred and thirty years later, does not invalidate a covenant previously ratified by God, so as to nullify the promise.)

6. "Manna from Heaven" for the purposes of both allegiance testing and in the unlikely event of food shortages inside the AB. (Exodus 16:4; Then the LORD said to Moses, "Behold, I will rain bread from heaven for you; and the people shall go out and gather a day's portion every day, that I may test them, whether or not they will walk in My instruction.")

7. *Redemption from breaking the moral law by blood sacrifices of unblemished animals.* Some people are a little uncomfortable with this, but it's a beautiful cross illustration. You see, the UT is so fragile that even one "false positive" can sacrifice everything, i.e., one sin upstairs, might sacrifice every *unblemished thing.* Therefore, what better way to convey the gravity of this fragility to the evaluee's, then by blood sacrifices of unblemished animals—for *their* sin. Remember, if any part of an evaluee is "darkness," how great is that darkness? (Exodus 12:5-11; Your lamb shall be an unblemished male a year old...the congregation of Israel is to kill it at twilight...it is the LORD'S Passover.)

8. *(My favorite) The tree of the knowledge of good and evil in the middle of the Garden of Eden symbolizes the pervasive Free Crown, in the space colonies.* The tree was needed to test everyone's will to power, in

the most unavoidable fashion possible. ***Why else would God allow the serpent into the Garden of Eden in the first place—even before the "Fall of Man"?*** (Genesis 3:4-5; The serpent said to the woman, "You surely will not die! For God knows that in the day you eat from it your eyes will be opened, and you will be like God, knowing good and evil.")

9. Demanding faithfulness. This tests everyone's deepest propensities under the guise of anonymity. Normally, people do not invite pain or ambiguity into their life unless the anticipated gratification of the UT outweighs it. (Hebrews 11:6; And without faith it is impossible to please Him, for he who comes to God must believe that He is and that He is a rewarder of those who seek Him.)

10. The use of a "Messiah" to show the evaluee's an up-close and personal example of successful holy living. (1 Peter 2:21; For you have been called for this purpose, since Christ also suffered for you, leaving you an example for you to follow in His steps.)

11. The use of a wide variety of temptations to enhance moral grappling. If you want to test a kite, you have to fly it against the wind to see how it holds up. If you want to test the propensities of the evaluee's, you must fly them in the "winds of temptations." If they can't stand up to the minor enticements inside an AB, they will never be able to handle the unavoidable, insecurable, major temptations in the UT—such as the Free Crown. (Luke 8:13; "Those on the rocky soil are those who, when they hear, receive the word with joy; and these have no firm root; they believe for a while, and in time of temptation fall away.")

12. ***The use of parables and analogies.*** We can't explain to the evaluee's in plain language, what our philosophical need is for the AB's. Nevertheless, we must give them some guidelines about how they can enter the UT and that's where the use of parables and analogies come in. For instance, we can't convey the problem of the Free Crown, but we can convey the parable of the

rich young ruler found in Luke 18:18-27. We can't convey the problem of no security and no laws in the UT, but we can convey the analogies of righteousness and justice found in Matthew chapters 5-7 and 23. Parables and analogies act as necessary surrogates.

13. The use of the concept of repentance to give everyone a second chance. It takes time for the average person to "find themselves," i.e., what they really want out of life. Sometimes the first road taken turns out to be erroneous. Therefore, it is only prudent for us, to be a little patient and grant everyone the opportunity to find his or her own unique comfort path. For some, this will ultimately lead to Angelicalness and the UT. (Luke 17:3-4; "Be on your guard! If your brother sins, rebuke him; and if he repents, forgive him. And if he sins against you seven times a day, and returns to you seven times, saying, 'I repent,' forgive him.")

14. The UT Captain and messengers playing ***"hide and seek" to foster anonymity***. Figuratively speaking, this technique gives everyone enough *virtual rope* to "hang" themselves—if they so choose. I.e., if the cat is away, the mice will playing—unless they are inclined not to. Some people believe that God doesn't play "hide and seek" with us. Well, no idea was more *irrational* to me during my many years as an atheist then this. I would simply point out that God seems to be one of only a few who don't have a web site. Why is that? (God needs to replace Heaven's Marketing Director.) Who wouldn't want to see live streaming video of Paradise and all the Angels? I'm not being entirely facetious. (John 16:25; "These things I have spoken to you in figurative language; an hour is coming when I will no longer speak to you in figurative language, but will tell you ***plainly*** of the Father.")

15. The use of brief glimpses of the UT. Sometimes it's a good idea to allow the *gossipy and literary evaluee's* to get a quick peek upstairs. I.e., glimpses of the lion lying down with the lamb (Angelic Love), the streets of gold and precious gems, no more crying, no more weeping

and no more tears. This information will spread among the evaluee's which will aid in deepening and widening the spectrum of temptation testing. (Revelation 21:2-4; And I saw the holy city, new Jerusalem, coming down out of heaven from God, made ready as a bride adorned for her husband. And I heard a loud voice from the throne, saying, "Behold, the tabernacle of God is among men, and He will dwell among them, and they shall be His people, and God Himself will be among them, and He will wipe away every tear from their eyes; and there will no longer be any death; there will no longer be any mourning, or crying, or pain; the first things have passed away.")

16. The creation of a "church" for believers to gather and talk about the Filter message. This will aid in providing comfort, shelter and a softer transition to those evaluee's who choose to become believers. (Acts 16:5; So the churches were being strengthened in the faith, and were increasing in number daily.)

17. *The requirement for evangelism.* This tests everyone's propensity for regeneration and reciprocation, i.e., there must be a desire on the part of the selectee's to become future UT facilitators (those who want to support and grow the UT.) How else can this attribute be determined downstairs, but by testing everyone's adherence to the commandment to evangelize others— especially strangers. (See Page 86 for more on this) (Matthew 28:18-20; And Jesus came up and spoke to them, saying, "All authority has been given to Me in heaven and on earth. Go therefore and make disciples of all the nations, baptizing them in the name of the Father and the Son and the Holy Spirit, teaching them to observe all that I commanded you; and lo, I am with you always, even to the end of the age.")

18. *A period of Great Tribulation at the end of the age.* This is inevitable at the end of every AB cycle, because of the feeding frenzy created by greedy people, trying to don the Free Crown. The book of Revelations and other Biblical references are sufficiently figurative

enough to accommodate many end time scenarios. (Revelation 13:16-18; he causes all, the small and the great, and the rich and the poor, and the free men and the slaves, to be given a mark on their right hand or on their forehead, and he provides that no one will be able to buy or to sell, except the one who has the mark, either the name of the beast or the number of his name. Here is wisdom. Let him who has understanding calculate the number of the beast, for the number is that of a man; and his number is six hundred and sixty-six.)

19. *A Second Coming event.* This signifies the useful end of the current AB testing cycle. (Matthew 24:29-30; "But immediately after the tribulation of those days the sun will be darkened, and the moon will not give its light, and the stars will fall from the sky, and the powers of the heavens will be shaken. And then the sign of the Son of Man will appear in the sky, and then all the tribes of the earth will mourn, and they will see the Son of Man coming on the clouds of the sky with power and great glory.")

20. *A Throne of Judgment* where all the selectee's, from that particular AB testing cycle, are chosen for the UT. (Revelation 20:11-15 Then I saw a great white throne and Him who sat upon it, from whose presence earth and heaven fled away, and no place was found for them. And I saw the dead, the great and the small, standing before the throne, and books were opened; and another book was opened, which is the book of life; and the dead were judged from the things which were written in the books, according to their deeds. And the sea gave up the dead which were in it, and death and Hades gave up the dead which were in them; and they were judged, every one of them according to their deeds. Then death and Hades were thrown into the lake of fire. This is the second death, the lake of fire. And if anyone's name was not found written in the book of life, he was thrown into the lake of fire.)

Coincidence or Design?

These 20 parallels of soft evidence do not constitute an objective proof for God's existence. We must subjectively decide, individually, if they are mere coincidences or if they are the work of a designer (e.g., God or a transcendent intelligence) and if so, is this designer still active today? There is no wrong answer to these questions, which we can know now (*perhaps by design*).

Those of you who anxiously want to live in an Angelic environment like Heaven, don't need 20 parallels to believe the Bible. Conversely, no amount of soft evidence is going to convince those of you, who have no interest in being Angelical, to waste any time on these parallels.

However, if there really is a God and we are inside his AB, we can understand ***why*** he would set it up this way. ***He wouldn't want to provide us with hard evidence***, but instead he would want to test us, via anonymity, to determine our deepest desires. He would want to test us to see if we are prepared to believe his message by faith, and become selected for his UT.

Therefore, philosophically speaking, the ambiguity of these 20 parallels, rules out nothing—*so, the playing field is always level, for both positions.*

To help you to understand this reasoning a little better, consider the *skeptics analogy.*

Skeptics Analogy

Imagine you are a minor league baseball pitcher and I'm your catcher and we are getting ready to run out onto the field at the start of a new game. You turn to me and say, "I don't see any big league scouts in the audience, so I'm not going to throw very hard today." I reply to you,

> "Well, just because you don't see anyone wearing a T-shirt that says, '***Hi, I'm a Big League Scout. Look Sharp!***' doesn't mean that they are not in the crowd. *Scouts deliberately attend these minor*

league games, anonymously. Their reasoning is, if they want to see the ball players in their natural state, they can't announce their presence before hand. Otherwise, all the players would run around like a bunch of yo-yo's, trying to be noticed for the upcoming draft. Everyone knows that no player can sustain that energy level throughout an entire big league season. Eventually they'll come crashing back to the Earth and be forced to play in their *natural state.* The question is this: do they have any talent in their natural state? Well, the easiest way for these scouts to find out the truth is by watching these minor league games, anonymously."

You then turn to me and say, in classic skeptic fashion,

"If I can't see them, they can't exist—period!"

I respond,

"Go right ahead and believe that if you want to. Frankly, the scouts would prefer that. If they're out there watching you pitch and they think you're big league material, they will approach you after-wards—in some fashion. If they don't think your big league material, you'll never even know that they

were up there watching you. Either way, they can't lose. This is not about you; it's about them. ***You should learn to trust people to do what is in their own best interests, even at the expense of your best interest."***

You walk to the pitcher's mound and mutter to yourself,

> "Gee whiz, I would really, really love to know whether or not, a scout is in the audience, but I don't know. However, I can understand now why they might attend these games anonymously. I can even imagine myself becoming a big league scout—ten years down the road; after my pitching career is over. However, now I'm forced to have to wrestle within myself as to what I'm going to do about this ambiguity, because I have only soft evidence of their possible attendance. I see no hard evidence and they may have deliberately set it up this way."

Meanwhile, up in the stands, a true big league scout is sitting there—incognito, watching you grapple on the mound. He knows that eventually you must throw the ball. At some point, the game has to start.

You see, everyone at some point in their life is going to have to "pitch" (even the atheists, theists and the skeptics). You could be walking down the street one day and a person comes up to you, beseeching you for a dollar. What are you going to do? **You have to make a moral decision—you have to pitch.** Do you flip him a nickel, a dime, a dollar? Do you pretend to be deaf and ignore him altogether? Do you provide him with a creative excuse or give him your verbal treatise on libertarianism, etc.

When you think about it, we all have to make dozens of unavoidable moral decisions everyday and that's what defines our *"pitching style."* God could be anonymously watching everything as **Heavens scout**, trying to determine whom among us (if any), is Heavenly League material. **The fact that the skeptic can't understand God's motives is irrelevant, because it doesn't bother God in the least.** He knows that *nobody* can claim ignorance on Judgment Day, because *everyone* will have a very long definitive pitching record. Remember, how you *perform* down here, is how you will want to *perform* upstairs, *because that's your natural self or state.*

(It is generally accepted that no one can acquire sufficient energy reserves to pretend to be someone else—indefinitely i.e., to adopt a different "moral compass" than that which is their own.)

Omniscience

As you may have gathered, the skeptic's analogy presupposes that God is not omniscient. After all, why would an all-knowing God need to be incognito about anything?

The question of omniscience can be addressed in two ways. First, I can invoke amber, which is to say that God's mind is omniscient and that his ways are perfectly rational, but well beyond the scope of my wisdom and imagination. Therefore, I simply have to accept it solely on the basis of faith. I don't have omniscience so I can't rule out the validity of this possibility. If it is true, then I may as well "check my brain at the door," because there is no further need for reasoning or rationality—vis-à-vis Religion.

Secondly, I question the concept of omniscience because it creates many practical and seemingly intractable problems. Two in particular come to mind.

1. If God is truly omniscient, then he has **nothing new to learn,** i.e., no more *Eureka!* moments for God. He is forced into a state of absolute predictability—similar to watching an endless TV re-run for the rest of his existence. His life becomes one big bore as exhibited by the protagonist in the 1993 Hollywood movie, Groundhog Day. Personally, I wouldn't wish this on anyone—let alone God.
2. **Omniscience requires finitude.** E.g., Suppose I asked you to measure the *true* radius of the Universe. You grab your tape measure, jump into a rocket ship and blast off into space, in one collinear direction.

    If the Universe is truly infinitely big, you will *never* return to me with a measurement. However, I can't rationally construe by your prolonged absence that the Universe is infinite—only that it *might* be infinite. Conversely, if you do return to me with a measurement, I will ask you, "what was the outer barrier to outer space?"

Hypothetically, you reply,

"Well, I first ran into a planet; beyond that, a void of space; beyond that, another planet and another void of space. Finally I hit an *impregnable wall,* proving the Universe is truly finite."

I will then ask you,

"If the wall was impregnable, then how do you know for sure that the wall is not infinitely thick? You see, if the outer barrier is infinitely thick, then the Universe can still be infinitely big; As a result, your finite measurement failed to answer the question. This kind of philosophical conundrum was self-evident, even before you blasted off."

In fact, I can't even conceive of what evidence is possible to conclusively prove that the Universe is infinite or finite. This is beyond my current imagination. In any event, if one can't prove finitude, one can't prove that they are omniscient. Mere finitude by premise is insufficient. A God of "practical or limited omniscience," doesn't have any of these problems.

I'm reminded of Deuteronomy 13:3; "...the Lord your God is testing you to find out if you love the Lord your God with all your heart and with all your soul."

If he needs to test us, maybe it is because he doesn't already know everything about us, i.e., our mind maybe a bottomless infinity, just like empty space and possibly beyond God's ability to completely read. (Hence, his need to set-up AB's on us.)

A Simple Model

In keeping with this train of thought, the simplest model for understanding God happens to be one based purely on pragmatism. Obviously, God could be far more advanced than this model, but it may not be necessary—vis-à-vis from our perspective. (*This is only the absolute minimum scenario to maintain rational cohesiveness.*)

Consider for the moment, that the very long path that our civilization has been on, is not the first time that our species has been down this road. **(Fig. J)**

Paths of Civilization

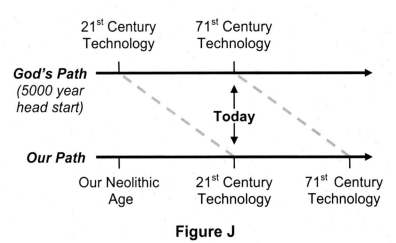

Figure J

For example, many of our modern day conveniences were in general use by the 21st century, such as the modern computer and the Internet.

Just suppose that another parallel civilization of humans, labeled God's path, invented the exact same conveniences 5000 years ago. Imagine them, taking the same basic social evolutionary path which we have taken—but with a 5000 year head start. **Where would their civilization be today?** Well, roughly speaking, they would be at the same technological level today that our civilization will be in the 71st century. Therefore, today:

1. They would be using highly advanced sciences, technologies and philosophies.
2. They would be living in space colonies.
3. They would have trillions upon trillions of femtotechnology robots and bountiful planet-sized robots.
4. They would have reached their Free Crown Point (FCP) and survived it, by creating a two-tiered social structure based on Angelicalness.
5. They would be using AB's the size of the Earth.
6. They would be currently testing their AB evaluee's, to determine who, if any, are Angelical.
7. They would have their AB's populated with femtosized video cameras and microphones recording and evaluating everything in real time.
8. They would manage their AB's indirectly using a Filter philosophy exactly like our Bible.
9. They would periodically send down messengers to regulate the moral buoyancy of the AB's, similar to that of our Biblical prophets.
10. They would try to develop a longevity machine and if successful, they would promise eternal life to all their chosen selectee's—because it is in their best interest to do so.

Does any of this sound familiar? You see, the first time our species would have taken this long path, it could have been completely secular and to go from that world view to an understanding of God, is as easy as *falling off a log*.

All you have to do is shift our existing path back 5000 years and then visualize exactly where we would be today. *God becomes one of us*, i.e., a living ancestor, who just happens to be super-human—only because he has had longer to work on it. We, with our primitive know-how can't distinguish between a 5000 year old God-man and the proverbial Omni-God, i.e., omniscient, omnipotent and omnipresent.

You see, **the concept of God need not necessarily be complicated.** I don't feel that there is a need to have to invoke the absolute realm to understand Judeo-Christian Theology. We simply need to ask ourselves a very sobering question and this is the crux of the issue. **Are we the kind of species that would be willing to build AB's on ourselves, when and if the need arises, at our Free Crown Point ?**

The answer is Yes!, because we see the precursors all around us today, e.g., bait cars, spy satellites, wireless intercepts, street surveillance camera's, predator drones, laser listening devices, U2 fly-over's, cell phone camera's, big league scouts, electronic eavesdropping equipment, good cop/bad cop interrogations—to name but a few. **We are already doing it to ourselves, incrementally. So why should anyone be surprised if we have gone all the way by now?**

If we can accept that God is much more technologically advanced than we are, then why shouldn't we acknowledge that he might be much more philosophically advanced as well? Anonymity can be a very powerful philosophical tool, when dealing with the unpredictable nature of provisionally bottomless minds.

Heaven

What is the *"Way of Life"* in Heaven? Well very briefly, if we continue to follow this simple pragmatic model (*the minimum scenario*), Heaven maybe nothing more than a highly advanced civilization of human beings living in space colonies called, God's Kingdom, with the following character-istics:

1. Like any standard UT, there are no security measures in place and nothing is enforceable. God has no wish to self-inflict the pain of having to administer a *police state* for the benefit of the non-Angelical. (John 8:36)
2. Like any standard UT, Angelic Love is the only cur-rency in their society. It was the necessary sacrifice on the "altar" of the AUD. (1 John 3:14)

3. Like any standard UT, material wealth is of no interest to anyone, because everyone has access to trillions upon trillions of servant robots to service their normal material needs. (Mark 10:23-25; Luke 21:1-4)

4. Like any standard UT, an expanding sphere of self-replicating robots is sent out to Terraform other inert planets into new AB's for human habitation and evaluation. (Rev. 10:5-6)

5. Like any standard UT, a symbolic Free Crown sits over in a corner collecting dust because no one has any desire to wear it. (Rev. 4:10-11)

6. Like any standard UT, the selectee's volunteer for numerous positions to maintain and grow the UT (Kingdom). (Rev. 14:1-5) **God doesn't want guests upstairs, he wants custodians.** Only custodians are willing to volunteer.

7. God sits on his Throne, adjudicating the inevitable *gray areas* that will arise in his Kingdom. (Rev. 21:7)

8. Collectively, their society has a far greater amount of knowledge about the Universe than we have—but they are not omniscient. (2 Kings 20:1-6, Gen. 6:6-7)

9. God's Love is so intense that it permeates every fiber of every selectee. (John 14:23)

The Way of Life in Heaven is basically to explore and to grow God's Kingdom, for the following reasons:

1. *More creativity.* God may have the same creativity dependency that we all have. He can only get so much from his robots because they can't "learn" anything that has not been presumed, by their inventor. Whereas most human beings abound with creative potential—given our provisionally bottomless mind. (John 15:11).

2. *More friendships and beauty.* Provisionally speaking, **the Angelical are the most precious individuals in the Universe.** They can't be fabricated like robots, only *cherry picked* through a long-term AB Filter process (Rev. 20:3).

3. *Enhanced self-preservation.* Philosophically speaking, if the Universe is infinite, it could contain other civilizations or kingdoms unknown to God (Isa. 44:8). At their Free Crown Point they would adopt either:

> 1. A two-tiered system based on Angelicalness.
> 2. A system based on continuous Dictatorships.
> 3. Collapse and implode away into extinction.

Rogue Dictatorships are problematic to God's Kingdom because they can:

> 1. Grow very large populations.
> 2. Deploy AB's with their own "weird and wacky" filter philosophy.
> 3. Brainwash most of their AB/UT selectee's into supreme loyalty and faithfulness.
> 4. Create an army of "heartless and callous," self-replicating robots.
> 5. Seek, plunder and pillage other civilizations in the larger "jungle" Universe. Their maxim being, "annex or be annexed."

In order for the Dictatorial civilizations to thrive they must stay competitive, which means they must foster creativity. The Dictators can certainly rely on their own creativity which is trustworthy, and then surround themselves with trillions of devoted pre-programmed robots. However, these robots have a very limited "creative" potential. For the Dictators to improve their overall situation, they must entrust their best technology to the creativity of some of their selectee's or other "trusted associates"—so they can improve upon it. However, in so doing, they may inadvertently give up their Crown through a *coup d'états*, made possible only because of these new creative improvements—in the hands of their false "trusted associates."

This proverbial **Catch-22 problem** doesn't exist in the Angelical civilizations because of their mutual love. They are extremely cohesive and collaborative, which will naturally produce the most fertile ground, with which to develop the best possible technologies. This gives Angelical civilizations a huge advantage in the jungle Universe.

Question: To stay competitive, wouldn't a Dictator then want to circumvent their Catch-22 problem by masquerading as an Angelical god to their dedicated selectee's? And if so, what is the easiest way to smoke them out?

Answer: Well, depending on their level of aptitude it maybe impossible. The best approach is to look at their overall level of transparency. A true loving God would have anticipated this concern and taken the proper steps to squelch it, as early as possible, e.g., by offering all his selectee's full access to himself.

Jesus said in John 17:20-21;

"I do not ask on behalf of these alone, but for those also who believe in Me through their word; that they may all be one; even as You, Father, are in Me and I in You, that they also may be in Us, so that the world may believe that You sent Me.

It wouldn't be very realistic for us to insist that, there will be **no creativity without transparency.** We would only be hurting ourselves, given our own creativity dependency.

The general rule is that, an imposter will place a higher premium on their own skepticism than on Angelic Love—so simply look for the telltale signs of distinction.

Please Note: All AB Filtration systems require a lot of time to yield genuine selectee's. This process can't be rushed (unless and until it becomes necessary).

For instance, In Rev. 20:2-3

"...the devil...would not deceive the nations any longer, until the thousand years were completed; **after these things he must be released for a short time.**
(...possibly for "extra-fine" filtration activities.)

CHAPTER 6

Summary with Conclusions

*"I have never let my schooling
interfere with my education."*
Mark Twain

The quintessential role of the philosopher is to try and build an evermore comprehensive and cohesive model of reality. To accomplish this, they must be willing to step back and passively inspect their surroundings in ever-greater detail. (This includes inculcating abstract notions such as: infinity, transcendency and a clear perspective on the future.) Only then, can they begin to contemplate various hypothesis to explain the nature and limitations of their newly derived knowledge—with the fewest possible exceptions.

They freely concede that during this construction phase, consequential and sobering conclusions may emerge. This is nothing new. It's merely a commonly accepted, unavoidable, *occupational hazard* that no one relishes. (In fact, the larger and more meticulous one's model, the more disquieting it is likely to become among its contemporaries.)

For me, determining **what has Ultimate Relevance** has been tolerably analogous to dissecting an *insatiable onion*. No matter how many layers of reality I peeled back, there was always yet another one of equal majesty. In hindsight, I learned the hard way that there is currently no evidence to rule out the possibility that the Universe might be infinite (topless and/or bottomless). As such, **there maybe no definitive answers to any ultimate questions.**

This condition may change over time. For instance, one day we may find evidence that the Universe is actually finite, before proceeding on to the acquisition of certitude and finally setting free all the hidden knowledge in the Universe. However, in all practicality this scenario could take decades, if not millenniums to reach its full fruition. Unfortunately, in the meantime, other events will transpire which will tend to overshadow this pursuit.

Case in point, shortly we (and our descendants) will be clamoring to colonize the rest of the planets in our Solar System. This will undoubtedly usher in the problem of the **"Free Crown Point"** (or FCP), *if not sooner.* **This event will clearly assume Ultimate Relevance**, provisionally speaking, within our practical realm.

Whether you subjectively choose to be an atheist, theist or skeptic, we are currently headed straight for the FCP, much like the Titanic steaming towards the infamous iceberg. This fact will become unavoidable after we have settled down in outer space—where we will have trillions of hopelessly indifferent and virus prone, self-replicating robots—*waiting for new instructions.* (This scenario is only one of many that can be used to illustrate the FCP problem. It's the flash point of our growing susceptibility to evermore-advanced Hi-tech tools, falling into the wrong hands. Bear in mind that, by nature, negative creativity is hopelessly unpredictable.)

As such, our emerging Space Age will develop into the Age of Utter Defenselessness (AUD)—where everyone will be at the mercy and pleasure of everyone else. This will drastically alter our social and political landscape because, **either the Crown will be worn by someone—or not.** Either we will have a Dictator of the Solar System and all of the vagaries, which that implies, *or we will choose to adopt a two-tiered solution to preserve our freedom.* This freedom option employs:

1. Anonymity Biospheres (AB) for covert containment, evaluee ethics testing and filtering.
2. An Upper Tier (UT) where Angelic Love is the only currency. It is mandatory because without absolute trust upstairs, there can be no lasting stability.

3. A Filter Threshold (FT) where the line of demarcation is drawn between the evaluee's and the selectee's.

In the beginning, ***the selectee's will be those who are completely enamored with the concept of Angelic Love towards all those who are like-minded—sight unseen.***

Somberly, we must accept the fact that this arduous choice will not be easy or unanimous, because Angelic Love is clearly not everyone's "cup of tea." However, we are entering into a new time period where the old 20th Century conventional mindset will no longer be a survivable option. As in the past, there will be no desire to put the genie back in the bottle or to uninvent certain technologies (even though they are completely dwarfing us).

This AB Filtration process is not based on prejudice, but instead on testing ones innate adaptability to survive each other in the new environment of the space colonies. E.g., Mount Everest has nothing against dolphins; they are simply not well suited for "mountaineering."

On a side note, let's be honest, I suspect that those who are not enamored with Angelic Love would be bored in the UT, anyway (unless they could wear the Crown). They would feel much more *at home, downstairs* in the *"spin cycle,"* with its unique brand of frivolous mirth. This is why we should encourage everyone inside the AB to do the honorable thing in life and "find themselves," as soon as possible.

Working Example?

To help to substantiate the merits of this AB/UT solution, I felt I had no choice but to delve into the subjective realm and drag the Bible into this argumentation. After all, I would be completely remised in my duties as a philosopher, if I failed to mention the existing soft evidence of a possible working example of this solution—*in action.*

The Christian Bible provides 20 major parallels with the AB Filter Philosophy (See Page 38). Some feel that this "connection" is merely a coincidence, while others believe it is not. ***Neither side can objectively proof their position.***

The latter group would suggest that this shows that God (the ultimate source of the Bible), at one time, decided to employ an AB on us. (In fact, the more I extrapolated the future, the more of this type of evidence came to light.)

This realization will always be received as **Great News** to any true selectee, because an honest AB evaluation is not something that they can setup on themselves. They need a third party to perform this unparalleled test, *covertly.* That's why the Bible/AB Filter philosophy maybe the greatest gift we could possibly receive downstairs.

Subjectively speaking, God could be:

1. A transcendent creator (this is the orthodox position).
2. A transcendent intelligence(s) who discovered the Earth and its various civilizations many years ago and decided to convert it into an active AB.
3. A human ancestor(s) who has been down this FCP road before (See Page 49).
4. Alive and well today, fostering his anonymity upstairs in Heaven.
5. Ready to return to the Earth to usher in his Kingdom (i.e., second coming), so we may never see the FCP.
6. In a different galaxy today, never to return—after having setup this possible AB.
7. Etc.

We really can't distinguish between our true history and our possible "staged" history (perhaps by design). Either way, we should assume the worst and go with what we've got. If the AB solution was good enough for God to initiate long ago, then it should be good enough for us—today. What difference should it make if the Bible is thousands of years old, if the source was thousands of years more advanced, at the time of "authorship." If it can guide us into solving our impending FCP problem, then I say, *"Let's use it."* (Even an atheist or skeptic could reasonably subscribe to this position. On balance, it is possible to be an apologist for the AB/UT solution, without sounding like, or even being a Christian evangelist.)

Parenthetically, I have to admit that by revealing all this soft evidence, I maybe unintentionally *pulling the curtain back on Heaven*, and introducing a new common sense perspective on Christianity. After all, **my philosophical model explains WHY God does, what he does, from a purely philosophical viewpoint**—assuming he exists. However, this discovery is unavoidable in every AB cycle, as it becomes more sophisticated over time. (If it was not unearthed by me, then it would have been by someone else.)

If there really is a living God deploying AB's and UT's, then **his selectee's have assumed Ultimate Relevance,** because they are the only items down here that God wants.

Personal Note

To be expected, I learned a lot about myself and what I really want in life from my long journey. I discovered that:

1. I am afflicted with a deep craving for the Angelical. They are so "off the charts" beautiful to me, that I think of them as **Chocolate Kryptonite.** I have even gone so far as to hang prints of Renaissance Angels on every wall in my home, because I love to kiss their feet while dreaming of the real thing in Heaven.
2. I have a desire to gravitate towards the Angelical, whether they are upstairs, downstairs, or yet to be discovered or born (and even if I never get selected for any Upper Tier). I can't explain this feeling, nor have I determined its origin. Nevertheless, it is real, even if this relegates me to a minority status.
3. (Conversely, I feel somewhat remote towards the non-Angelical, but I want them to know their options.)
4. I feel compelled to reciprocate by becoming an AB/UT facilitator. This is what has motivated me to author this book. (A chance to be a kind of point man.)
5. I couldn't detach myself from the art of philosophical deliberation and reflection—if I tried. It runs too deep into my soul. Luckily, I only need the usual recliner, park bench, cemetery, and a computer to assist me.

6. I recognize that everyday we are getting a little bit closer to the FCP. Therefore, ***time is on my side*** (up to a point).

So, the next time you see a news story on television about an evermore sophisticated, humanlike robot, ask yourself this basic question:

> "I wonder how long it will be before this family of robots will be programmed to self-replicate?
> After all, every company has an incentive to cut their production costs and what better way to accomplish this, but by "enslaving" their product line to manufacture more of itself."

You see, on the day when self-replication is finally reached, the triumphant company won't care about their stock price anymore. They will simply launch their robots to the Moon, auto-manufacture a few trillion of them, and then declare themselves as ***The Only Remaining Superpower***. On that day, your freedom will be hanging by a thread (unless the proper early steps are taken).

Action Items

To avoid this fate certain preliminary actions can be taken (assuming God doesn't intervene first). Since we are only at the ***Hearts and Minds stage***, I recommend the following:

1. Acknowledge the Free Crown Point (FCP) problem.
2. Acknowledge the coming ascendancy of Angelic Love as the only currency that can survive itself in a free space colony.
3. Discuss and analyze the philosophical merits of all solutions to the FCP problem, including the two-tiered option of AB's and UT's.
4. Consider the option of adopting the Christian faith.
5. Don't panic—be yourself.
6. Visit **markplain.com** for more information.

Questions and Answers

"You can tell whether a man is clever by his answers.
You can tell whether a man is wise by his questions."
Naguib Mahfouzr

1. How much stock should we put into scientific knowledge given the fact that there have been so many revisions over the years?

The history of science is replete with many corrections and revisions in many areas. These occurrences are to be expected, as we slowly grope towards certitude.

I would put a lot of stock in scientific knowledge—but only in the practical realm. The absolute realm, dealing with such things as the origin of life, the origin of the Universe and issues surrounding fundamental premises (etc.) are best left to the philosophers—since they have a deeper understanding on the *limitations of knowledge.* For instance, I'm always fascinated by scientists who have these very long illustrious mathematical equations for defining the absolute realm, e.g., the grand unified theory of everything, the size of the Universe and the odds of life evolving by accident. It's obvious that if one of the variables in their equation happens to be an infinity or an infinitesimal, then their entire equation becomes indefinable and therefore of what use? If their equation doesn't have any infinities or infinitesimals, then what bearing does it have on the real world, and therefore of what use? So as long as the Universe *might* be infinite, its deepest nature maybe beyond mathematical explanation. I'm not suggesting that the Universe is infinite or finite, only that there is not enough conclusive evidence to rule out either one.

Back in the 1970s there was an interesting slogan which was, "follow the money." (This was in connection with the Watergate conspiracy.) Today the catch phrase in science should be "***follow the premise.***" Everyone should realize that every scientific conclusion ever decreed was based on some premise(s). Therefore, the validity of any conclusion can be no better than its weakest premise.

As one digs deeper and deeper into the fundamental premise of science, they will invariably run headlong into the Philosophy of Science. Once there, they may ask themselves a fundamental question: is it possible for the Universe to be infinite? *Not is it necessary—but is it possible?* If they believe that it is possible, then they must also concede that it is also possible that they possess only an infinitesimal insight into this infinite Universe. Therefore, it would be irrational to ascribe any absolutes upon this infinite Universe, from only an infinitesimal vantage point.

Also ask yourself these questions:

1. Is it possible to have a fundamental scientific premise that is not a dogma? If not, would such a premise not be deemed hopelessly subjective?
2. Why would one persons hopelessly subjective dogma be anymore objectively true, than anyone else's hopelessly subjective dogma? Based on what criteria?
3. Does knowledge even have an objective criterion when it comes to premise? How does one prove it?
4. Is not the fundamental premise of science, predicated on the fundamental premise of knowledge?
5. What premise(s) is the *edifice of science* currently resting on today? Should we be worried?

You see, these questions (and others) illustrate why the discipline of science desperately needs much stronger philosophical oversight.

When scientists stick to their *own knitting* they do a great job. The problem arises when they *wander off the reservation* into the absolute realm and bring their dubious premises with them, e.g. all that has been seen, is all that can exist. (This premise has reeked havoc.)

In all fairness, I think an argument can be made that this predicament is more a case of **abdication by philosophers** (who generally would rather not *monitor* scientific reasoning) rather than **activism by scientists**. After all, there are still too many people who consider the Philosophy of Science, to be an oxymoron.

2. Is the head of a pin flat?

This question is actually a philosophical Rorschach Test; it's designed to assess your cognitive depth perception. Some people will answer this question, "No silly, the head of a pin is not flat—it's a point, otherwise it wouldn't be able to sew through clothes."

Others will answer, "Yes, under an electron microscope, the head of a pin is categorically flat." While still others will answer, "indeterminable, because its true head ultimately vanishes into the possible infinite ingression of empty space."

Therefore, if you are asked this question on a school test, gauge your answer based on the course curriculum. If it is a Home Economics test, answer no; if it is a Physics test, answer, yes; and if it is a Philosophy of Science test, answer, unknown. In the practical realm, truth is in the "amber" eyes of the beholder.

3. How does one prove that matter can truly annihilate in a Universe that might be bottomless in all directions?

The short answer is they can't. Too often when particle physicists build bigger and better particle accelerators, they find smaller particles of matter that they didn't think existed before. (Maybe these particles have been around for eons.) It is safe to say that the general premise of, "all that has been seen, is all that can exist," has never been true in hindsight.

Nevertheless, let us consider the archetypal fission experiment with a proverbial Uranium 235 sample. After it undergoes fission it produces "spent fuel" (Strontium-90, Cesium-137, etc.) and various forms of energy (radiation, heat, etc.). We have been told by many physicists, that the mass of the spent fuel is less than the original mass of the Uranium sample. This difference in mass has been con- verted to energy, hence, they believe that this constitutes a proof for the "annihilation of matter" ($E=mc^2$).

However, *how do they know that they possess all the possible spent fuel?* (Is there a difference between, all that has been seen and all that can exist?) For instance, is it possible that the fission event produced such incredibly tiny particles, that they simply faded from everyone's view? Is it possible that by the next millennium, we will have "super- duper" accelerators that can find all these so-called "missing" pieces of matter—at higher magnifications? What evidence is there to rule out this possibility?

Answer: *No Evidence. If space is infinitely divisible, there will be infinite room to misplace an infinite number of infinitesimal particles—all having some mass.*

It's undeniable that the process of fission produces vast quantities of energy, but does matter have to annihilate in order to produce that energy? Is that the only de facto possibility? That's the real crux of this question. So, here is an alternative scenario.

When I was a child, my friends and I would play a game called "Battle Tops." We would wrap a string around these small plastic tops and place them into this concave board. At the count of three, we would all pull our strings like a ripcord and the tops would go off spinning around this 12-inch board. Eventually they would drift towards the center where they would collide. All of a sudden, we would hear a Ping! as one of the tops went sailing across the room behind the couch. *It was great fun.* But, that experience reminds me of a possible fission scenario.

You see, at closer inspection, a Uranium 235 nucleus could contain an infinite number of tiny spinning autonomous subatomic particles, like tops—minding their own business. When a neutron is introduced in a specific way, it initiates the fission process. This maybe nothing more than initiating a cascading series of collisions, that converts rotational kinetic energy, into linear kinetic energy—*without annihilating anything*—just like Battle Tops.

When you think about it, there are many other possible scenarios for the fission energy source, besides annihilation. (I only need one alternative to call this dogma into question.) *Therefore, until we can philosophically distinguish between "too small to detect" and annihilation—we cannot objectively prove that anything has ever truly annihilated.* It is yet another scientific conclusion, based on a dubious premise. (This one maybe the most pervasive *sacred cow* in science today).

4. Doesn't Planck's length define the smallest possible volume of empty space?

Planck's length is based on the notion that empty space is quantized and not continuous, i.e., it rules out the possibility that empty space is infinitely divisible—by premise (as determined by empiricism). However, this creates a problem of circular reasoning.

Philosophically speaking, in order for empiricism to have any relevance—vis-à-vis the absolute realm, one must assume a prior, that all that has been seen, is all that can exist. *But, that is exactly what is at issue here*, e.g., why should anyone trust the calibration of a caliber, that had been used to calibrate itself. Objectivity requires a third-party reference.

On the other hand, if empty space is infinitely divisible, then the Universe is bottomless in all directions, i.e., infinite. All our empirical wisdom would have only an infinitesimal insight into this infinite Universe. Consequently, we maybe *drowning* in uncertainties and therefore unable to prove the validity or probability of quantization.

This is why the issue of fundamental premises is so important, i.e., if one's foundation is "out of plumb," then so will everything else that is resting upon it.

5. What is the answer to Zeno's paradox of motion?

To simplify the basic tortoise paradox, picture a number line with two endpoints labeled zero and one. **(Fig. K)**

You place a particle at point zero and decide to move it towards point one, timing the duration of motion with a stopwatch. For each cycle, you start the watch, move the particle half the remaining distance, stop the watch and then record the time. Imagine performing these series of cycles over and over again.

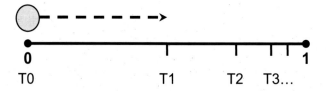

Time	Extra Distance Traveled
T0	0.0
T1	0.5
T2	0.25
T3	0.125
T4	0.0625
T∞	0.000000000...

Sum Total - 0.999999999999...

Figure K

Hypothetically speaking, if empty space is infinitely divisible, there would be an infinite number of points between any zero and one; therefore, these cycles could be repeated indefinitely. You would be constantly moving the particle closer and closer to one—but never quite reaching it. You would also be constantly starting and stopping the stopwatch, adding more time.

Consequently, some have argued that motion can't exist because it would take an infinite amount of time to move any particle, any distance. What is the answer to this apparent paradox?

Well, any particle in motion maybe passing over an infinite number of infinitesimal points, taking only an infinitesimal amount of time at each one. The sum total of an infinite number of infinitesimal numbers is not necessarily infinity. It may simply be a number with an infinite number of non-zero decimal places, but still less than one.

The deeper question is this: does the empirical observation of motion presuppose a bottom to empty space? Well, if empty space is truly bottomless, then under every video microscope with an ever-increasing shutter speed, we will forever empirically observe the particle taking quantum leaps. I.e., the particle existing at one point and then at a different point on the next frame. But, does that mere fact make it conclusive, that empty space is bottoming-out? Answer: not necessarily.

We have no idea what is going on inside the infinitesimal realm. We are no more perceptive of infinitesimal time than infinitesimal space, so at the present we can't rule out any possibilities. In the final analysis, motion itself maybe just as mysterious as human consciousness. It may tell us much more about our own innate perceptive limitations, then anything else.

6. Can time exist without motion?

Is a motionless Universe, a timeless Universe? This is really an abstract philosophical question. Time is basically a human invention to describe relative motion. Empty space and matter maybe able to exist without time as long as they remain stationary. It is currently impossible to prove that empty space is ever in motion, and therefore time and space maybe mutually exclusive. This is because all our current motion detectors require a collision at some minuscule level—which requires mass—*which empty space doesn't have.*

Bottom line, our Universe maybe an infinite volume of permanently fixed empty space that is oblivious to matter and its motion.

7. What is Freewill?

No one knows all the mysteries of human consciousness and its attributes. Freewill is an abstract phenomenon that best reveals the limitations of our knowledge. For example, imagine you are sitting in a stationary train and looking out the window at another person sitting in a different stationary train. As you are watching them, all of a sudden, you start to detect relative motion between the two trains. For a split second you are unable to distinguish whose train is actually moving, or if both trains are starting to move—relative to the ground. Therefore, any witnessed phenomena, may have a lot more to do with the state of the observer than the observee.

Similarly, we can't distinguish between having a freewill and being ignorant of being thoroughly pre-programmed robots. In the absolute realm, **omniscience is the only thing that freewill is sure to be free of**; therefore we can't currently prove its existence.

Incidentally, I do agree with the general operating assumption that people should be held culpable for their decisions and actions despite all these ambiguities, other-wise anarchy would descend on our society.

8. What general advice is there on "finding oneself"?

Philosophically speaking, most people eventually "finds themselves," but I would start as early as possible and *avoid the rush*. For the most part, we seem to be hard-wired to maximize pleasure and minimize pain in our life. Everyone defines these slightly differently, based on their own distinc-tive desires, interests and values. Therefore, it is always best to chase after your unique passions and "tickle" them.

For some, this will involve becoming an inventor, or a gardener, or an athlete, or a philosopher, or a nurse, etc. You need to ask yourself a very selfish question: what do I really want out of my life? Who really an I?

Answering these questions requires deep introspection, so it's best to get a critical distance on everything. This is where the phrase "to take-off and find yourself" comes from. You know what your parents want you to want with your life, and you know what your friends and siblings want you to want. We all know what *"Madison Avenue"* wants us to want, but what do you really want for yourself? What specific activity will elicit the greatest overall pleasure? Most of us have a general idea, but if you are still unsure, here is my advice.

Visit the largest public library in your area. I guarantee you that if you lightly peruse every book in the library, some area of interest will jump out at you. Make a note of it and continue looking, because there maybe yet another subject (which somehow got previously overlooked), that will elicit even greater pleasure. Unfortunately, most people stop at the first pleasure subject that they find and they don't discover the other delights until years later and then find themselves having to make a career change. Don't let that happen to you. Doubt your "*pseudo-omniscience*" and glance at every book in the library.

When you have finished, your passion subjects may seem insignificant at first—don't let that bother you; as long as they give you a tremendous sense of inner bliss. So much so, *that you can't imagine spending your life engaged in anything else.*

Doing the thing you love will never be considered a job or work. It will always be a timeless and a rewarding experience that leads to an overall happy life. Hopefully it is something that you can make a living at.

Remember, **Utopia is a verb—not a noun.**

9. Which is worse, living in a Universe of certitude or incertitude?

As long as it is possible for the Universe to be infinite, there will always remain an element of uncertainty. Therefore, we can't know the definitive answer to this question.

However, some may argue that the biggest drawback to a Universe of incertitude is all the anxieties that it generates from all the mysteries—real and abstract. For instance, is our species groping around in a dark Universe all alone, or are we part of a quasi-ant farm for someone else's cosmic amusement, or are we being cultivated by some discriminating aliens to become Horderve's at their next house-warming party? The possibilities are endless, but that doesn't mean that we should live in fear of the unknown. Instead we should be prudent with what we strongly believe—that we do know.

On the other side of the coin, my current conception (which may change) of a Universe of certitude is somewhat bleak. For instance, there is nothing new to learn in this type of Universe, so after a while everything becomes a boring re-run. Even worse, is the knowledge that every particle in this finite Universe will have been mapped down to its trajectory, velocity, spin and mass. As such, this type of Universe will have only a finite amount of kinetic energy. This energy level will slowly diminish to zero over time due to all the future head-on particle collisions.

Therefore, the ultimate fate for a Universe of certitude (again, from within my amber), is *purposeless permafrost*. It may take a long time to get to this point, but we will be forced to watch re-runs in the interim.

I think the best way to handle this question is to simply not ask it. *No seriously.* We should realize that the Universe doesn't owe us anything. It doesn't owe us certitude or incertitude. Accordingly, we should adopt a happy-go-lucky attitude and appreciate life one day at a time, free from anxiety. (This is incidentally, the reason why I believe that philosophers have the fewest number of attachments or distractions—vis-à-vis modernity.)

10. Does quintessential non-intelligence really exist?

Many people believe so when they, for instance, look at a stone. However, if we could look deeper and deeper into the structure of any stone, we may find infinite complexities such as orbiting electrons, electromagnetism, strong and weak nuclear forces and gravity.

Strictly philosophically speaking, it is impossible to prove that these phenomena are not signs of intrinsic intelligent life forms—especially since these manifestations are beyond our technological ability to perfectly replicate. It could be argued that, *this evidence may constitute a proof for the existence of intrinsic intelligent beings that are smarter than we are.*

For instance, consider the spectacle of ocean tides. When I'm down at the beach I sometimes ask myself, how does our Moon make the oceans rise and fall? Scientists can predict tide water levels and gravitational forces, but they don't know in detail, how or why gravity works. E.g., how any specific water molecule is mindful of the Moon's existence from a quarter of a million miles away, through the relative vacuum of outer space? Are there tiny strings connected to both? Are there femto-sized life forms from within the water molecule, orchestrating this behavior?

I know this may sound a little outlandish, but if matter has no fundamental particle—how can we rule out any possibilities? Maybe gravity is *their* way of trying to communicate to us. Maybe they are waiting around for us to "smarten up and think outside-the-box" (and maybe we will someday).

You know, we humans have a distinct history of not recognizing and appreciating genius in its lifetime. It's on record; it's undeniable. Individuals like Vincent Van Gogh and Edgar Allen Poe, never got the credit they deserved during their lifetime. We should acknowledge and accept our blind spots, at least long enough to think more creatively. We shouldn't assume that our technology is the *best possible technology in the Universe*, especially since we may have only an infinitesimal insight into our possible infinite cosmos.

11. Since we have already discovered the MAD doctrine, haven't we therefore already reached the Free Crown Point (FCP)?

The MAD (Mutually Assured Destruction) doctrine is a derivative of the Cold War, whereby each Superpower knew that the other Superpower had full retaliatory capability to any first strike. Therefore, any offensive action taken would at best only ensure mutual destruction.

Nuclear technology has indeed proliferated over the years. Fortunately, to date, this type of "launch decision" is reserved to a very select group of levelheaded world leaders. A Terrorist group may decide to compromise our nuclear security structure, but there is no sign of it yet.

The Free Crown is very different because it can't be secured due to the unpredictable nature of negative creativity, e.g. computer viruses. ***Therefore, it will be freely available to anyone, anytime, once we arrive at the AUD*** (which we haven't reach yet. At a minimum, the AUD requires a new technology to be invented such as self-replicating robots, designer pathogens, etc.)

No one knows how much longer our "window of opportunity" will remain open before we reach the FCP. Prudence demands that all solutions be put forward now. Remember the dictum of the AUD, "whoever happens to have the biggest and best technology, can dictate all the rules."

12. Isn't the use of Anonymity Biospheres (AB) an invasion of privacy on the evaluee's?

There are many ways to approach this question because there are many angles from which to look at it. For me, I've yet to hear a good reason why anyone needs privacy from the "Angels." (Remember, all the selectee's in the UT are Angelical.) I can readily accept why many people want privacy from telemarketers, email spammers, etc.—but not the Angelical. (Unless, they happen to be up to no-good).

13. Aren't the people inside the AB's entitled to the best Upper Tier (UT) technology?

The answer is no. There is no evidence that the Universe owes anyone, anything. Even the Hi-tech countries of the world, currently don't share a lot of their highly-advanced technologies with the Third world. This is due in part to a number of legitimate security concerns. For instance, if nuclear material ever fell into the hands of a rogue warlord, it might create a worse situation for everyone. Handing over the Free Crown to the non-Angelical is just as irresponsible.

14. Isn't there always going to be an element of uncertainty in the UT selection process, regardless of which criteria are implemented?

The provisional answer is yes. Obviously, incertitude forbids us from knowing that we have eliminated all risks. However, we can and should maximize our safety margins by using AB's and selecting only Angelical individuals (at least until a safety net is constructed). My hope is that long-term stability can be achieved before and if certitude is ultimately attained.

The general rule of thumb about risk assessment is the more an evaluee hungers for Angelicalness:

1. The more they will pine after the UT and all its chosen selectee's.
2. The more detached they will become from their world and "worldly" things.
3. The more transparent they will be about their own personal failings.
4. The less encumbered they will allow themselves to be over the rituals of the AB.
5. The fewer regrets they will have, if any, upon arriving upstairs.
6. The less nostalgic they will be for the past, after they arrive upstairs.

7. And most importantly, the least willing to compromise and the most willing to sacrifice for the UT.

Unfortunately, risk assessment requires much greater scrutiny, which is well beyond the scope of this book.

One thing is for sure though; everyone, no matter where they appear on the Values Scale (See Page 36), will want the Filter Threshold (FT) placed just below their name.

15. Will there be sex in the UT?

For our very first batch selection, I recommend selecting celibates only. Once we have installed a safety net (See Page 30), we can then play around with all sorts of different entrance criteria, without risking harm to the second level.

Those evaluee's who choose to be celibate inside the AB's carry limited sexual baggage or sexual tension into the UT. Whereas, those evaluee's who choose to be sexually active are more difficult to evaluate, because they raise these additional questions:

1. Will they respect the autonomy of others in the UT who want to say "no" to sex? E.g., Will they demand a million concubines? (Remember, nothing upstairs is enforceable and there is no place to run or hide.)
2. Will people want to couple like a 1960s commune? Will this coupling lead to possessiveness, jealousy, envy and strife—like a 1960s ex-commune?
3. How will they behave away from their possible spouse and family, who may still be inside the AB? They may not even know the answer to that question. After a month or two in the UT, they may become homesick and decide to go back, which may disqualify everyone in the entire AB cycle, depending on how much information is divulged about the day-to-day operations upstairs and the AB hidden equipment.
4. How will they react if their spouse isn't subsequently selected? Will they have a tendency to nominate their spouse or form a conspiracy with others along the

lines of, *only if you nominate my spouse, will I nominate your spouse?*

5. Will they be more inclined to nominate younger, sexually attractive or sexually active evaluee's instead of the Angelical?

6. What is their added propensity to compromise the integrity of the UT, solely because of their sexual desires?

You see, the answers to all these questions will not necessarily appear on their Anonymity Biosphere Tapes (ABT), which makes their selection much more complex (but not impossible).

To lower the overall risk, I think it's a good idea to employ the "Odd Person Hypothesis," (The theory which states that unmarried people are capable of carrying out the best, most dispassionate decisions in crisis situations.)

Why should we voluntarily and unnecessarily imperil our species, right out of the starting gate—before the safety net is operational? *Let us never forget, sex communes claim to fame is not their longevity.*

16. How can an evaluee keep the commandments of spurning evil and loving their neighbour as themselves, if their neighbour happens to be evil?

Those evaluee's who are selected and moved into the UT, are going to be meeting an ever-growing population of strangers. *They will have to be predisposed to falling deeply into Angelic Love with all of them from minute one—sight unseen and without exception.* Without that assurance a priori, they would never have been selected in the first place. (Remember, Angelic Love is the only currency upstairs.)

How can one test for this attribute inside an AB if not by adherence to the Love Commandments. You see, if you love your neighbor as yourself, you will never enslave your neighbor because no one ever enslaves themselves or those whom they love; therefore, they can be trusted upstairs.

This doesn't mean that we must embrace everything downstairs, or that we must love everyone exactly the way they are, *necessarily.* Instead, to love them or give them some benefit of the doubt for what they might become— namely Angelical.

Our neighbors' may not appear that way in the beginning. Nevertheless, we can gently prod them to deeply examine themselves. We can quiz them on what their deepest aspirations and utopian ideals are—free from coercion. (Take into account, it can take years for the average person to "find themselves," so patience is a virtue.)

Incidentally, the church is full of personal testimonies from individuals who freely concede to living an unscrupulous existence in early life, but eventually changed their direction. (If God permits U-turns, then maybe we should as well.)

17. What is the fate of the evaluee's who are not selected for the UT?

Technically, there can be many different fates apart from just leaving them inside the AB. The full list of options largely depends on the level of technology available at "Punt" time. (See Page 27)

I don't feel it is very fruitful to spend a lot of effort discussing day-to-day AB operations, because if we don't punt for a generation or two *or three*, many of our current designs and ideas in this area will have become obsolete.

We are currently only at the *"Hearts and Minds"* **stage**. As a result, I'm much more concerned with the broader philosophical issues, because they are the first hurdles that must be overcome.

18. Does the sign of our existence conclusively establish the veracity of Intelligent Design?

The provisional answer is no. There are currently five general scenarios for our origin. In brief;

1. We are the product of a completely freak collision of nature's particles, with no purpose.
2. We have always existed in some form or fashion, coming from eternity past (if only as a consciousness in the shape of a sub-atomic matrix).
3. We were created by a transcendent intelligence or a series of transcendent intelligences, which came from eternity past.
4. We are only an hallucination, devoid of any real existence. We just don't know it yet.
5. We sprang from "nothingness."

The bottom line is that we maybe living inside an infinite Universe, topless and/or bottomless, in all directions. Consequently, we might be drowning in uncertainties, so there is currently no way for us to figure out the probabilities for *any* of these origin scenarios. **We just don't know how much we don't know.** Therefore the jury maybe forever out on this issue. When and if we ever discover certitude, we will first need to prove that the Universe is finite.

As a result, I sometimes wonder if too many scientists, philosophers and other intellectuals waste too much time focusing on the absolute realm. ***Staring at infinities all day doesn't have Ultimate Relevance!***

Metaphorically speaking, some thinkers associate themselves with the men of the Santa Maria who manned the sails on their trip westward in 1492. Others are partial to the observers on the high mast, staring at the horizon all day for signs of land. I feel a good "seamen" should do both—not either/or. To be a *relevant thinker today,* one should "work the sails," by focusing on providing practical solutions to our pressing practical problems and only periodically look up at the "horizon" to see if infinity is still gawking back at them.

> **Please Note: Some of the following questions make the assumption that Heaven and God exist and that we are inside his AB.**

19. Why have you focused more on Christianity, to the exclusion of other Religions?

As a skeptical rationalist, I have two big concerns about Religion in general.

1. ***Anyone can start a new religion.*** They don't need any money, property, references or even an education. (In fact, if they were homeless it would probably add to their mystique.) The tenets of their religion can be vague and self-contradictory. They can get away with this by simply invoking amber, i.e., their theology maybe irrational to us, but not to a deeper mind—namely the mind of their god.

    They will point out that our opinion of their god can be no larger than our imagination; therefore, we can't refute their tenets from within our own amber. We simply have to accept it or reject it, solely based on faith. Thus, many religions can operate on their own rules of evidence, which is why they can take on a life of their own. (I think if one wants to start a new religion today, the only thing they need is an ego.)

2. The complete lack of ***shopping around.*** Most people are *very picky* consumers when it comes to cars, clothing, furniture, appliances, houses, spouses—but not religion. Sadly, many still allow themselves to be stuck with the religion which they happened to be born into. All to often, ***religion has become more a consequence of geography, rather than reason.***

As such, it is very difficult (if not impossible) to be a rational and cohesive apologist for all religions.

Christianity is very different because it uniquely has 20 parallels between its sacred text (the Hebrew Bible and the New Testament) and our future AB Filter Philosophy. This makes the complete Bible both a distinctively historical and futurist book, at the same time.

20. Did God create his own consciousness?

The Bible states that God's consciousness was never created; rather that it came from eternity past (which is consistent with the AB Filter Philosophy). Modern day common sense might argue that God must first say I exist before he can say I will create. Therefore, he couldn't create his own existence.

More importantly, if God's consciousness can come from eternity past, then consciousness itself can come from eternity past, *including possibly ours.* God could have fashioned a "suitcase body" around our core consciousness, much like constructing a jumbo jet around a core pilot. God's "airplane" is designed to fly, but only we (the pilot) can decide where it shall go.

This makes perfect sense to me, because it immediately explains why God uses AB evaluations. He doesn't already know what kind of "pilot" we are, because he never created the pilot, just as he never created his own pilot or consciousness.

Does this reduce God to the status of a U.F.O. or little green man? The answer is no. I think it defogs God to a level of rationalism that we can understand and respect—with no paradoxes.

There are many instances in the Bible where God encourages us to think rationally about him, such as Isaiah 1:18; "Come now, and let us reason together," Says the LORD.

21. Are there any contradictions between science and the Bible, i.e., the fossil record vs. a young Earth?

I don't see any contradictions because we really don't know enough about our origins. However, there is a much deeper philosophical perspective on this issue which you should be made aware of.

A persons idea of their god can be no more descriptive than their imagination, so if one has a shallow imagination, they will inevitably be a meager advocate for their god. Consequently, it should come as no surprise that these "lesser deities" flounder, when they are confronted by the so-called *"expertise"* of the natural sciences. I.e., they create all sorts of unnecessary contradictions, such as the fossil record.

What do we really know for sure about our fossils and where they came from? Parenthetically, if we build our own AB's in the future, I have little doubt that we will deploy all sorts of artificial "**fossil props**" into the artificial soil stratums. The reason being, when the naive inhabitants find these "fossils" by "accident," they will undoubtedly jump to the wrong conclusion; that their world is millions, if not billions of years old, when in reality it is extremely young.

Fossil props are the single best idea to maximize the appearance of anonymity inside the AB's—bar none. It would be foolish for us not to use them in the future. For instance, how many used car dealers would roll back the odometers on their used vehicles, if they knew that they could get away with it? Why shouldn't we tinker with the chronometers on our own AB's—if it's to our own advantage? After all, we are only providing a little more disinformation to the evaluee's, above and beyond the existing pile of con-cealed data.

Similarly, God could have terraformed this planet in six literal days, a few thousand years ago, using a trillion, trillion self-replicating femto-robots. (Notice, my description of my God isn't limp.) These tiny machines could have easily built and planted all our so-called "fossils," for the sole purpose of us finding them and jumping to the wrong conclusions. Namely, that God doesn't exist, or that God flew the coop, or that God is not necessary. Either way, God achieves his objective which is anonymity—just like a big league scout craves anonymity. It might require 22nd century technology for us to finally empirically prove it to ourselves, e.g., detect a pico-sized serial number on a so-called "Tyrannosaurus tooth." But long before then, this AB may recycle—so God's secret is always safe with him.

You may be wondering how would God know that we would jump to the wrong conclusions, a priori? Well, the Earth maybe only one of a million AB's throughout God's domain and possibly on its 10th cycle. Therefore, God (the pragmatist) could have easily predicted our current path, based on his experience with numerous prior AB cycles.

(It should be pointed out that there are countless other scenario's for our "true" history, e.g., God could have discovered this planet and its civilizations by accident, a few thousand years ago and decided to convert it into, yet another, active AB, etc.)

You see, depending on your imagination, God could be playing all of us like a "fiddle" right now, and whatever so-called "evidence" there is to the contrary, I can always invoke fiddler, i.e., God specifically set it up that way to foster his own anonymity. It is very easy to *fiddle* with people, who can't see their own cerebral myopia. Philosophically speaking, it is only the ones who are humble enough to invoke amber—who are also smart enough to invoke fiddler. (This may not be a coincidence.) In Matthew 11:25-26; Jesus said,

> "I praise You, Father, Lord of heaven and earth,
> that You have hidden these things from the wise
> and intelligent and have revealed them to infants.
> Yes, Father, for this way was well-pleasing in
> your sight".

Translation: In Heaven, heart trumps brain, i.e., what good are intellectuals if you can't trust them with the Free Crown. Quasi-Mother Teresa types can be trusted and whatever else they may offer us is *sweet gravy*. We should trust God to do what is in his own best interest.

Bottom line, **God or no God, fossil props and other dating type props, all foster greater anonymity inside the AB's that wouldn't otherwise be there.**

22. Will the evaluee's inside the AB's be given any religious materials?

The evaluee's will be given information and materials having to do with entrance requirements into our UT, as part of our overall AB Filter Philosophy. However, they won't be given any extra religious material, because the facts on the ground suggest that, God may or may not exist, whereas Terrorism and Megalomania clearly do exist—therefore they should get top priority.

Allowing multiple so-called "sacred texts" and multiple so-called "deities" inside the AB's only gums up the works during the UT selection process, because it creates **dueling standards.** That's why indigenous false deities and their philosophies won't be tolerated either (at first).

However, let us not forget that our criterion for entrance into our first UT is basically the same as the Judeo-Christian God's criteria for entrance into his UT (Heaven). **If it's sauce for the goose, it should be sauce for the gander.**

This raises an interesting question. Would God dishonor our Angelic selectee's for not knowing the name of Jesus— through no fault of their own? This question reminds me of the millions of people living outside the Middle East during Christ's earthly ministry. Most of them never got a chance to meet Jesus—let alone hear his Gospel message, due to mere geography. Does that mean that they were all condemned to Hell Fire, for being born in the wrong place? Or will they be judged individually, based on their own conscience? I believe the latter, because as Abraham said in Genesis 18:25; "...Shall not the Judge of all the earth deal justly?" Also in John 14:6; Jesus said, "I am the way, and the truth, and the life; no one comes to the Father but through Me." Jesus is referring to Angelicalness and not in some artificial belief in his historicity, e.g., William Shakespeare or Julius Caesar.

Bottom line, I believe God would fully understand our predicament and won't condemn our selectee's for knowledge to which they have not been given access. Our justification for our first AB is not unlike God's justification for *his* first AB.

This raises another interesting question. Does this answer condemn me to Hell Fire for a lack of faith, if I'm not prepared to roll the dice on our entire species, i.e., on the hope of Christ's universal redemption, even under the state or risk of a Megalomaniacal dictatorship? *Now that's a Great Christian question.*

Put it this way, figuratively speaking, I subjectively believe that strawberry is the best flavor of ice cream, despite the fact that I can't objectively prove it. Similarly, I subjectively subscribe to Christianity, but I can't objectively prove that God exists. It is perfectly permissible for me to roll the dice and bet my own soul, but that's the outer limit of my comfort zone.

I believe in limited omniscience, therefore, I also have to concede that it is *possible* that Heaven could have met with an unfortunate accident, two thousand years ago, and we have yet to hear about it. As such, it would not be prudent for us to put all our *eggs in one basket*. But instead, should the need arise, be prepared to build our own AB's in the future instead of exclusively waiting around for God's second coming and possibly allowing the next want-to-be Dictator to grab the Free Crown.

Becoming preoccupied with the politics of "soul gambling" will lead to complacency and may forever close our "window of opportunity," to maintain our free society.

In all honesty, I have been wrong many times in the past and *I currently don't have the luxury of claiming to irrefutably know, that I can prove God's future salvation.*

23. How does God derive his sex standards?

Some have argued that the selectee's in Heaven don't have a sexual libido. They are typically referring to Luke 20:34-36;

> And Jesus answering said unto them, "The children of this world marry, and are given in marriage: But they which shall be accounted worthy to obtain that world, and the resurrection from the dead, neither marry, nor are given in marriage: Neither can they die any more: for they are equal unto the angels; and are the children of God, being the children of the resurrection."

Our sexual libido maybe nothing more than an AB utility designed for the purpose of "driving us" to procreate; Or a purely natural bodily function which God allows to let stand. Either way, it serves numerous objectives:

1. Sex is power, i.e., our libido can be used to test our will to power over others. This can be very telling.
2. It provides a way of bringing new core consciousnesses into the AB's for evaluation purposes, and in such a way as to not reveal any hard evidence for the existence of the UT, i.e., general anonymity must be maintained.
3. In the event of a birth, it prevents anyone from trying to escape the AB through the "front door."
4. In the event of a birth, it fosters the natural affections of two parents, who will subsequently have a desire to nurture the vulnerable new child. Family bonds also come into play.
5. In the event of a birth, it might generate an additional peculiar test over one's "allegiance to Angelicalness"; assuming other family members disapprove of it. Is spirit thicker than blood? This can be a very agonizing dilemma for some evaluee's to answer. Jesus said in Matthew 10:37; "He who loves father or mother more

than Me is not worthy of Me; and he who loves son or daughter more than Me is not worthy of Me."

The fact that our culture has turned sex into a Big Business doesn't mean that God must revise his standards. God allows for this industriousness, because it generates a plethora of temptations (which tend to greatly enhance moral grappling). God's motto might be, *"Better I should know the true "you" now, while you are downstairs; rather than afterwards—upstairs, where you may pose a threat to me."*

We shouldn't overlook the "commonality of power" linkage between sex and the Filter Threshold. This is why sexual purity is so prized, both upstairs and downstairs.

Parenthetically, I remember a high school gym class I once attended years ago, where all the guys were talking about the subject of marriage. To my amazement there was unanimity, that we would all be sexually promiscuous until the age of 25, and then settle down and get married—but she had to be a virgin. (This was apparently the *new math* in those days.) No one batted an eye; we all thought it was perfectly reasonable and appropriate that she, above all, should be pure. I suspect this sediment is still somewhat true today among many male high school students.

I never forgot that poignant moment, because it made me realize that our species places a higher value on purity—all kinds of purity. This raises the rhetorical question, *why should those upstairs think any differently?*

24. When a child dies do they go immediately into Heaven?

The Bible states in Hebrews 9:27; "...it is appointed for men to die once and after this comes judgment." The Bible also states that God has the technology of resurrection and therefore it is within his purview and interest to send any evaluee's back to the AB's, if they have been *judged* to have not received sufficient testing.

25. Why should anyone bother to fix the world if it is only God's AB designed exclusively for testing evaluee's?

If there is a God and we are inside his AB then every material thing downstairs is a **virtual prop**, solely designed to test everyone for their desires. But that is a big "If."

If it is true, then we will never be able to create a perfect "Shangri-la" down here no matter how hard we try. Our AB administrators upstairs would never permit it, because it would lower the overall level of moral grappling inside our society. If we get too close, they could easily throw a "wrench" into the works, e.g., earthquakes or other "natural" disasters. Consequently, **we should expect "Hardball," and not "Mr. Fix-it," from the folks upstairs.**

Since we can't prove that we are inside God's AB, many people will invariably try to create a paradise, in the here and now, based on their collective utopian ideals.

In the final analysis, each person will have to determine how they want to play this. It's a truly subjective call. But keep two thoughts in mind; these ambiguities maybe **"by design"** and if you were comfortably relaxing upstairs right now, you may want to keep the status quo. After all, *Earth's currency is Materialism and Heaven's currency is Angelic Love. One realm craves the Free Crown and the other is repulsed by it.*

26. Why should anyone bother to evangelize the world if no "true positives" can ever be lost?

The answer is indirectly connected with the "Way of Life" in Heaven (See Page 52). God's request to us to evangelize others (especially strangers) downstairs, is not for the purpose of finding the true selectee's before they are "lost." But rather, God wants to smoke out our individual *proclivity* to want to find the Angelical, via their "surrogates." If one has no desire to "search for" and "gravitate towards" the Angelical downstairs, they will have no similar desire for it upstairs.

Consequently, they will tend to **refuse to volunteer** to become UT facilitators (if given the choice). If such were the case, many evaluee's (including possible future Angels) would have their AB testing and evaluations delayed, and so, for all practical purposes, "lost" (justice delayed is justice denied.) **All true selectee's want to reciprocate because it is the loving thing to do.** In fact, it has become the *Way of Life in Heaven.*

God's request for evangelism should come as no surprise to anyone, because **how else** can he test for our propensities towards the Angelical and the UT, but by *emulating the notion* of "souls being lost."

Keep in mind that God's need for anonymity, limits him to employing analogies and parables (surrogates) downstairs. This is why there are so many cookie cutter parallels between the Bible and the AB Filter Philosophy. **This is also why Christ's ministry was deliberately designed to be so brief and geographically confined.** God wants the *lump* of his evaluee's, to be *leavened* by their convictions, and not by the snap of his fingers (which is far easier to do).

In John 21:15;

Jesus said to Simon Peter, "Simon, son of John, do you love Me more than these?" He said to Him, "Yes, Lord; You know that I love You." He said to him, "Tend My lambs."

This was a universal instruction given to the church, which means, those who keep this commandment, will be helping to distinguish themselves as true selectee's.

However, to those of you who have read this answer and believe it, you might lose your incentive to evangelize again. How would this change ones evaluation?

Well, first of all, nowhere in my philosophical model do I claim to be able to prove that God's existence. So, I am merely elongating the spectrum between believer and non-believer (which is always a good thing). Secondly, God's test, namely "ones propensity for evangelism" would be replaced with a new kind of test called "ones propensity to gravitate towards the Angelical" (welcome to my world). *All AB cycles eventually reach this point of sophistication; intellectual maturing is unavoidable.*

Bottom line, *Christianity is about Angelic Love; Angelic Love wants to reciprocate via UT facilitation— false positives don't.*

27. If God is not omniscient then how can he guarantee us eternal life?

There are two ways to answer this question. First, I can simply invoke amber (See Page 47). Second, from within my amber, there are numerous instances in the Bible where God demonstrates that he has the technology of resurrection (Luke 8:49-56; John 11:1-44). This can be considered, in all practicality, as the same as the technology of eternal life.

For instance, I remember a TV advertising slogan, which was "Diamonds are Forever." This was in reference to the fact that diamond is the hardest known substance today. It is therefore considered permanent, for all practical purposes. The slogan need not necessarily be taking in absolute terms.

God's intention is for all his selectee's to live "*forever*," because it is in his interest to ensure that.

28. What is the answer to the Biblical freewill / predestination riddle?

How does God create a culpable freewill, foreknowing everyone's decisions without preordaining them? Well, this riddle or paradox has been around for many years and it's only one of many that arise from the concept of an omniscient God. However, *it is not a paradox to those who believe in limited omniscience, like myself.*

According to the Bible, relative to God, everyone will end up being deemed either righteous or unrighteous, just or unjust, sheep or goats. There is no third category. In Romans chapter 8 and Ephesians chapter 1, it states that God has predestined the righteous from all eternity to be saved, and therefore by process of elimination, he has *predestined the unrighteous.*

From within my amber, this is not a capricious act because he doesn't know conclusively, who the unrighteous are—yet. Our apparent freewill derives from the possible infinite ingressions of our mind, which maybe beyond God's ability to read and adequately predict. Therefore, God ultimately holds each of us culpable for the decisions that we choose to make.

29. What are the strongest verses in the New Testament that parallel with the AB Filter Philosophy?

Jesus said in John 13:34-35; "A new commandment I give unto you, That ye love one another; as I have loved you, that ye also love one another. By this shall all men know that ye are my disciples, if ye have love, one to another."

Love is critical to the success of the UT and mandatory for God's salvation.

♥   ♥   ♥

Jesus said in Matthew 5:10; "Blessed are they which are persecuted for righteousness' sake: for theirs is the kingdom of heaven."

Righteousness is critical to the success of the UT and mandatory for God's salvation.

♥   ♥   ♥

Jesus said in Matthew 5:48; "**Be ye therefore perfect**, even as your Father which is in **heaven is perfect**."

1 Peter 1:16; "Be ye Holy; for I am Holy."

Ephesians 5:27; "That he might present it to himself a glorious church, not having spot, or wrinkle, or any such thing; but that it should be Holy and without blemish."

Angelicalness is critical to the success of the UT and critical for God's salvation.

♥   ♥   ♥

Jesus said in Luke 18:25; "For it is easier for a camel to go through a needle's eye, than for a rich man to enter into the kingdom of God."

Pragmatically speaking, rich people are never repulsed by wealth and the power that it brings; therefore, they will never be repulsed by the Free Crown. Mere indifference to it is not good enough, because eventually they will become bored with that point of view. The only people who are consistently content to ignore the Crown are the Angelical.

♥   ♥   ♥

Jesus said in Matthew 6:6; "But you, when you pray, go into your inner room, close your door and pray to your Father who is in secret, and your Father who sees what is done in secret will reward you."

Everything we say and do inside an AB maybe recorded, so technically there is no such thing as *non-prayer*. However, God encourages this type of behavior, because those who pray alone in closets tend to speak openly, honestly, and sincerely—because there is no lasting incentive not to. Voluntary confessions are always welcome upstairs.

♥   ♥   ♥

Jesus said in Luke 8:17; "For nothing is hidden that will not become evident, nor anything secret that will not be known and come to light."

We really don't know, how much we don't know about the Universe, so we can't objectively limit God's technology, e.g., maybe ever hair on our head really is numbered (Matt. 10:30). God may have trillions of femto-technology cameras falling as dust on everything—all the time. As such, he maybe able to effortlessly, capture everything that goes on down here, inside this possible AB. There is no evidence to rule out this possibility and there are many good philosophical reasons to sanction it.

♥   ♥   ♥

Jesus said in Luke 16:10; "He who is faithful in a very little thing is faithful also in much; and he who is unrighteous in a very little thing is unrighteous also in much. Therefore if you have not been faithful in the use of unrighteous wealth, who will entrust the true riches to you?"

This verse is fairly obvious. If one can't be trusted inside an AB, then they won't be trustworthy in the UT with a pervasive Free Crown.

Also keep in mind that according to 1 Cor. 6:3 "Do you not know that we will judge angels?..." Why would God trust non-Angelical selectee's to properly judge potential Angels?

Answer: *He wouldn't trust them with this responsibility.* Only the truly Angelical can correctly make these types of difficult judgments.

30. What is God's Invitation?

God's invitation is his request to each of us, to start a long-term relationship with him and all his selectee's. Every union begins with each side taking a first step. Jesus said in John 14:1;

"Do not let your heart be troubled; believe in God, believe also in Me. In My Father's house are many dwelling places; if it were not so, I would have told you; for I go to prepare a place for you. If I go and prepare a place for you, I will come again and receive you to Myself, that where I am, there you may be also."

In this verse he is inviting us all to his Father's house in his UT, namely Heaven. In Revelation 3:20;

Jesus said "Behold, *I stand at the door and knock*; if anyone hears My voice and opens the door, I will come in to him and will dine with him, and he with Me. He who overcomes, I will grant to him to sit down with Me on My throne, as I also overcame and sat down with My Father on His throne."

The door he is referring to is the door of our heart. The "Angelic Love" that God is looking for, requires us to open that door, so he can enter in to this union with us (or oneness). This can't be coerced; it must be a voluntary, mutual act of our wills. In Matthew 16:24;

Jesus said to His disciples, "If anyone wishes to come after Me, he must deny himself, and take up his cross and follow Me. For whoever wishes to save his life will lose it; but whoever loses his life for My sake will find it. For what will it profit a man if he gains the whole world and forfeits his soul? Or what will a man give in exchange for his soul? For the Son of Man is going to come in the glory of His Father with His angels, and will then repay every man according to his deeds."

It is very easy to go through life as a *virtual clam*, seldom expressing our deepest feelings and beliefs. However, the moment one conveys their faith, they are opening themselves up to possible consequences. People don't naturally invite pain into their life, unless they believe the deferred gratification outweighs it. This is what separates the true believers (the selectee's) from everyone else. Therefore everyone should "examine themselves" (2 Cor. 13:5) and "count the cost" (Luke 14:28) to see if they are "in the faith" (Col. 1:23). If you are willing to make an informed commitment to Angelicalness and begin a relationship with God then I recommend reading aloud Luke 18:10-14. Jesus said;

"Two men went up into the temple to pray, one a Pharisee and the other a tax collector. The Pharisee stood and was praying this to himself: 'God, I thank you that I am not like other people: swindlers, unjust, adulterers, or even like this tax collector. I fast twice a week; I pay tithes of all that I get.' But the tax collector, standing some distance away, was even unwilling to lift up his eyes to heaven, but was beating his breast, saying, '**God, be merciful to me, a sinner!**'. I tell you, this man went to his house justified rather than the other; for everyone who exalts himself will be humbled, but he who humbles himself will be exalted."

These verses are commonly called the "sinner's prayer" and it is the best starting place to begin, before reading the rest of the Bible.

Glossary

Amber
> The finite amount of accessible knowledge (facts) that one has accumulated. Similar to a prehistoric insect encased in *amber* or trapped in time.

Angelical
> Kind and lovable persons who manifest righteousness, purity and selflessness.

Anonymity Biosphere (AB)
> Large terrestrial or space based habitat containing an isolated and self-determining community. All the inhabitants (the evaluee's) are raised in a very low-tech environment and kept unaware of numerous hidden cameras all around them, recording their every deed.
> The purpose of the AB is to test for each evaluee's deepest ethics and desires and only those who have been deemed worthy (the selectee's), will be secretively moved into an Upper Tier (UT). (See Page 24)

Anonymity Biosphere Tape (ABT)
> The audio/video (etc.) recording of each evaluee's life inside an Anonymity Biosphere (AB). This is used for evaluation purposes. For highly advanced UT's, each evaluee can be graded in real-time, i.e., no physical recording is required to be manually reviewed.

Age of Utter Defenselessness (AUD)
> The time period following the Free Crown Point (FCP) where everyone will be at the mercy and pleasure of every other individual. (See entry for FCP or Page 27)

Bottomless Space
>The concept that empty space is infinitely divisible.

First Encounter Strike Susceptibility (FESS)
>The breach susceptibility of a systems security, due to its inherent inability to predict all forms of human creativity, vis-à-vis all the new (unforeseeable) attack methods.

Filter Threshold (FT)
>The minimum value required for each evaluee to be selected for the Upper Tier (UT). (See Page 36)

Free Crown Point (FCP)
>The point at which a private entity possesses a technological innovation which is so advanced, that it can "forcibly" supplant all rival technologies, allowing the operator to declare themselves "Ruler of the Solar System." E.g. The invention of self-replicating robots. This event will usher in the new Age of Utter Defenselessness (AUD).

Intelligent Design
>The theory that suggests that the Universe is too complex to be the product of an unguided process, hence, an intelligent designer must have been involved.

Lower Tier (LT or Downstairs)
>The low-tech environment inside an Anonymity Biosphere used for testing evaluee's. (See Page 24)

Odd Person Hypothesis
>The theory which states that unmarried people are capable of carrying out the best, most dispassionate decisions in crisis situations.

Punt

> The difficult decision by the future political establishment to cut their losses and implement the two-tiered solution of Anonymity Biospheres (AB) and an Upper Tier (UT), to resolve their Free Crown problem. This category of solution will only be initiated after all other options have been thoroughly exhausted.
>
> In football, a very difficult coaching decision is when, in the final few minutes of a game, a team finds itself up by a few points, at midfield, with 4th down and inches. Sometimes, due to offensive injuries, the coach must decide to punt and give his defense a chance to win the game. (I.e., only after the overt schemes have failed, will the covert schemes of AB/UT be invited onto the playing field.)

Spin cycle

> The antics of life inside an Anonymity Biosphere (AB).

Stepped up

> The process of educating newly chosen selectee's in contemporary Upper Tier (UT) technologies and philosophies.

Surrogate

> One that takes the place of another; a substitute.
>
> Surrogates (both psychological and physical) are used extensively inside Anonymity Biospheres (AB), to proxy truths between the evaluee's and the selectee's upstairs. For example:
>
> 1) The Bible describes some analogies and parables (psychological-surrogates) to extract the deep values and desires of each AB evaluee, especially their "UT" attributes.
>
> 2) How the evaluee's behave toward righteous people *downstairs* (physical-surrogates) is how they will want to treat the other righteous people *upstairs*. etc.

Topless Universe
The concept that the Universe is unbound, i.e., no ultimate ceiling limitations.

Upper Tier (UT or Upstairs)
The area outside an Anonymity Biosphere (AB) used by the selectee's (or the chosen evaluee's). This will most likely derive from our first "permanent" space colony. (See Page 24)

UT Facilitator
Selectee's who want to support and grow the Upper Tier (UT). There will be numerous positions available from which they can volunteer for. They are all *driven* by Angelic Love.